LC

Prophets, Priests, and Politicians

Prophets, Priests, and Politicians

ALAN STREYFFELER

JUDSON PRESS
Valley Forge

PROPHETS, PRIESTS, AND POLITICIANS

International Standard Book No. 0-8170-0502-1
Library of Congress Catalog Card No. 71-129487

Printed in the U.S.A.

Dedicated to the faculty and former students
of Evangelical Theological Seminary
whose demand for theological reflection
and critical debate provided me
with the tools for coming to grips
with the problem of secularization.

Contents

Preface

The legacy of the learned pastor who is also a prophetic advocate of the people is a deep and venerable one. Although the church frequently hides this tradition from its own consciousness in favor of the sweet man who is cheaper than a psychiatrist, the tradition as it actually works out in the lives of people hinges in every decisive moment on those who engage in more than the mere performance of the priestly functions. This tradition depends on those who also discern the tracks of the divine in the midst of the pressing concerns of public life and do their best to restructure both church and society to be obedient to those marks. The early fathers of the church were often such men; so were the radical reformers, so also the separatists in England, and some of the great figures in American piety from Edwards in the eighteenth century, through Bushnell in the nineteenth, to Rauschenbusch and the early Niebuhr in the twentieth. These men were not primarily academic theologians, although they did their technical homework. These men were professional churchmen in every sense, but they refused to become functionaries of established practice or hacks of some Christian party line. They raised controversy at every turn, for they were alive to the human situation as they sought the presence of God in the midst of human existence. And they found it in quite unorthodox places.

Alan Streyffeler shows every promise of being in such a lineage. From his experience as a pastor in the turbulent bowels of Chicago, and from his superior work in graduate studies at Andover Newton Theological School, he has forged this book. The existential and academic points of departure have been joined in a practice that requires articulation and a theory that demands action.

The existential point of departure is the ministry in the soft underbelly of the greatest city of middle-America. Chicago, during the past few years, has reflected the successive crises of the nation in a peculiarly dramatic way. Martin Luther King faced the blatant racism in Cicero. Black militants were shot in an apparent act of repression. The defenders of law and order rioted against the young at the Democratic convention. A trial which entailed mockery of the courts by the defendants and mockery of justice by the court captured the attention of the world. Clergy who attempted to minister to the dispossessed were harassed. One was murdered. In the nation a war which many considered senseless prevented the cities from obtaining the resources to prevent decay. And corporations resisted even modest efforts to prevent their corruption of the environment. The great universities were in turmoil. In all of this, the role of being a minister — even a believer — was reshaped, expanded, redesigned until it approached a new understanding of what it means to be in Christ. To be a minister means not only visiting the sick and caring for the troubled. It means not only preaching and teaching and praying. It also means living from and for the people of God, from and for all those called out of ordinary life into a new enspirited community that attempts both to transform the destructive dimensions of society and to respond in celebration to the new possibilities at hand. And throughout, it means reorganizing the structures of the community so that they sustain rather than corrupt life. In short, it means becoming prophet, priest, and politician.

The academic point of departure is the summary, critical

evaluation, and constructive attempt to go beyond the "secular theology" of the past decade. The problem of trying to redefine the relationship of the secular and sacred dimensions of life is, of course, a long one, reaching back at least half a century. And the battles have been intense. At stake in all this debate are implied disputes over the relationship of symbol and reason, church and society, vertical and horizontal dimensions of experience, soul and body, salvation and history, and religion and world. The dominant conceptions of the relationship between the sacred and the secular are sorted through for their potential contributions to a viable community of faith in the future. The results point toward an alive political theology with a compassion for persons and a consciousness of transcendence.

But in several ways the present book takes on significance beyond the spiritual lineage and beyond the particular points of departure of the author. For it presents the sometimes confusing and occasionally confused, but ever fresh and strangely compelling, concerns of a new generation of young clergy.

The book is characterized by a linkage of theory and practice that demands transformation of ordinary patterns of piety and society. Yet it will not allow itself to become merely a new "radicaler than thou" sectarianism that lapses into the cynicism of some university-based radicals. The new generation of clergy are too close to the people for that. They demand restructuring of the Establishment, the redistribution of power, and the altering of priorities for righteousness' sake. But they recognize also that merely to be against the Establishment is not automatically to be for liberation and justice. They are caught between the contrary realizations that out of the old root comes the new shoot, and that new wine cannot be put into old wineskins. The new generation of young clergy are trying to steer the local congregations between the Scylla of despair over old loyalties and the Charybdis of disaster in trying to create all *de novo*. This book reflects a set of reconstructive concerns that is coalescing in the infrastructure of every denomination in every city. It will be heard.

This volume also reflects a life-style of engagement that obtains among the new generation of young clergy. Nor is it

merely activism that motivates them. Among the hidden assumptions of the generation, that here and there breaks forth
in this statement, is the presumption that God is a living God,
struggling, communing, celebrating, and tabernacling with
his people in the midst of life. God may be found for some
in the quiet meditations of the heart; but for this generation,
he is found in the abrasive power of conflict that exposes the
true loyalties of people and institutions, in action-reflection
seminars where new dimensions of humanization are revealed,
and even in committee meetings and coalition politics where
wider bonds of trust and wider visions of community are
hammered out.

And this book reflects a vital conception of theology. This
is a theologically concerned book, although it may not be
seen as such by many technical theologians. Discussions of
Sin, Salvation, Trinity, and Ecclesiology are not topically ar-
ranged or even explicitly stated, although they pervade the
substratum of consciousness out of which the generation
speaks. Theology in this mold is relatively disinterested in
maintaining certain classical polarities, and it can readily
draw together disparate sources to render new combinations
of insight. For theology is not seen as the end of the religious
quest nor the reversal of classical formula. Theology is a necessary instrument for dealing with the guts of life which is religious at its root. Theology is a way of looking at life, a con-
ceptual framework that allows us to see and to communicate
where in the midst of existence that ultimately worthy power
which we call "God" is moving.

This book, therefore, reflects the first major effort by this
promising young pastor to articulate the passions and conceptions of a generation. If the new reformation that has
been heralded for nearly a generation is going to take place,
much of the credit will be due to those who, like the author,
are prophets, priests, and politicians. We need more like him
and more of him.

MAX L. STACKHOUSE

Andover Newton Theological School
January, 1971

1
Strangers in a Strange Land

Are we really living in a world of permanent change? Our lives seem to be moving in a number of orbits which change as rapidly as styles of clothing. So many of our common experiences are like a class reunion in which the password is, "My, how you've changed!" The total human situation may be described as exposure to the strangeness of new things and the frightful queerness which has come into life.

We find ourselves involved in a world situation which threatens all that is secure and familiar. We stand at a point in the Western world where the acceleration of radical change and the massive reshaping of human institutions can only be matched by epochal shifts like those which occurred in the fifteenth and sixteenth centuries.

In the past man experienced his world as "nature" which both embraced and threatened him. His attempts to shape his world were insignificant compared to the seemingly unconquerable nature that was always bigger than he. Nature was his "bosom" and his "mother." But this nature which formerly embraced man has, through industrialization, become the object of attack by man.

Change has not been restricted to man's relationship to the world of nature, however. There is no human relationship — parent and child, husband and wife, worker and employer — that has not been touched by the strangeness of our new situation. The search in the past for precedents to guide us and wisdom to sustain us is frequently frustrating. We discover that there is no future in the past. The wisdom which we have received was meant for a simpler age and just does not fit into the complexities of our time.

The theme which captures the mood of the 1960's is provided by the lines of the folk ballad, "The times, they are a'changin'." Contemporary man is called upon to go more places, to be exposed to more things, and to come to grips with more issues than any one in previous generations. The staggering achievements in space exploration alone not only leave us at a loss for adjectives, but challenge us to develop a new understanding of our place in the universe. In spite of our desire to keep life familiar, we find ourselves at many points to be "strangers in a strange land."

The man of faith is by no means immune to the queerness or strangeness of the times. Indeed, he may discover that some of the most familiar theological positions and church practices have been called into question. Any perfect image of faith has been shattered like a mirror which has been roughly handled.

One of the assumptions which has been called into question during recent years is the belief that church attendance as an expression of faith commitment would continue to spiral upward. However, it now appears that a "recession" has set in. The searching probe of the researcher's pencil has brought this change to our attention. Recent attempts to discover what has been happening to the level of religion in the United States point out that religion has lost ground startlingly in the last decade. In 1957 14 percent of those polled in a Gallup national sample indicated that religion was losing its influence. By 1967 the figure had risen to 57 percent. In ten short years the proportion of Americans who saw religion in retreat had quadrupled. Let us consider how this change in attitude has been expressed in the local church. Many of those persons who indicate that religion plays a less crucial role in their lives might still be occupying the pew on Sunday morning. But the real test of their loyalty would come if a controversial issue to which they were opposed should be supported by the minister or the church. During the latter half of the 1960's such tests of allegiance came with great frequency. Probably the blow struck by James Forman has been the watershed of challenging issues faced by the church. His Black Manifesto has challenged the faith response of the church as well as her more sensitive financial interests. Regardless of the church's general refusal to respond positively to the Black Manifesto, she has obviously been shaken by it. The agenda of the world has been dramatically laid at her altar. Never again can the church claim sanctuary from the times.

Lest we jump to the conclusion that declining church membership and the financial squeeze are symptoms of the inevitable decline of religion, we must look carefully at the role which the church needs to play in the future. The real challenge to the man of faith comes not from the numbers of persons who are critical of the institutional church from within and from without. The real test comes in the challenge to the content of the church's faith. For example, unless we see the Black Manifesto as posing a serious faith question, we are not plumbing the depth of its challenge to church life.

In recent years the challenge of faith was most dramatically evident in the form of the "death of God" theology. Although the popularity of this movement may have seemed to be a flash in the pan, the depth of its challenge is as old as the church and as new as contemporary man's fascination with scientific achievement. Laymen who were previously disposed toward considering theologians as the custodians of the faith discovered that some theological professors were proclaiming that God was dead! Although the seminarian found the discussion to be "heady stuff," the untutored layman was thrown into a state of theological shock by the coverage of the death of God phenomenon in the mass media.

Those clergymen who found themselves unprepared to cope with the challenges of the death of God theology recognized their failure in their inability to cope with the contemporary trends and theological thought of the times. The challenge to the meaning and existence of God was but the most formidable of the symbols which have come under attack in recent years. The result is that the concerned citizens of the kingdom of God are finding it increasingly necessary to reevaluate the theological formulas and symbols of the church. Thus churchmen are being called to come to grips with the potential "credibility gap" which lurks behind previously unquestioned, central affirmations of the Christian faith. Change is at the top of the church's agenda.

The churchman who is sensitive to the impinging events of the times and who finds himself caught in the squeeze play between the church and the world has become aware of what may be heralded as the dawn of a secular age. Because the clergy have failed to prepare themselves or their laity for the implications of these changing times, we are faced with a legacy of threatened clergy, ignorant laity, malfunctioning church ministries, and a rampaging series of events and cultural movements difficult to interpret or accept. Before the church was even able to deal with change it had to deal with revolution.

The air is increasingly filled with anti-tradition missiles launched from both within and without the church. Even those missile bases which have been established inside the institutional church are primarily reflecting the urgency of the modern world whose challenge to traditional church life cannot be minimized. No given theological position or church practice is safe for long in even the most rarified of spiritual atmospheres. The increasing number of church leaders in even the upper echelon of the church hierarchy who are critically appraising the church is a prime example of this comprehensive challenge. When the winds of change have blown long enough through the styles of life and patterns of thought to which the church has been accustomed and to which the various symbols and formulas of the Christian faith have grown attached, then the man of faith may suddenly wake up to discover that he has been sleeping through a hurricane. This awareness of change has come to most church communities at one level or another.

Churchmen are discovering that many of the "sacred cows" of church practice and tradition which may have seemed indispensable to the church's life and mission are being called into question.

This awareness that the churchman must be sensitive to the relationship which his beliefs have to the world in which he lives was pointed out most sharply by theologian Rudolf Bultmann. Bultmann had the audacity to point out that, because the times in which we live are different from the world situation of Jesus, our understanding of the faith must change accordingly. The logic of Bultmann's thinking has stunned more than a few conscientious churchmen. It makes a difference, for example, that Jesus spoke to a people whose world was filled with demons, whose universe centered in Jerusalem, and whose theological system was dependent upon a pyramid of beings beginning with the lower form (man), proceeding through the angelic beings, and climaxing with God himself. Bultmann struggled to get behind this understanding of the universe in New Testament times so that the New Testament message might come through with a greater clarity and relevance for contemporary people.

This bandwagon which was given momentum by Bultmann a quarter of a century ago has been filled with countless persons who have considered the rise of science and technology and increased urban development to have rendered aspects of the Christian tradition obsolete and meaningless. The cosmology or understanding of the universe in any prescientific age, such as the New Testament times, has seemed incredible to modern man.

This process of the world "becoming worldly" has been most recently called "secularization." Since the late Middle Ages, slowly but all the more definitely and irreversibly, man, his society, his science, his culture, and his economy have moved out of the great all-inclusive edifice of medieval Christendom in which theology and the church possessed the key to every sphere of life.

For centuries theology had been able to lay claim to being the "queen of the sciences." The church was able to address the world with authority. But the erosion of the church's authority since the Reformation reminds us of the childhood game, "Button, button, who's got the button?" The authority to speak most meaningfully to the times and to give *the* interpretation of the world has passed like a button from the hands of the theologian to the hands of the humanist, to the historian, to the natural philosopher, to the political analyst, and eventually to the scientist. One need only be reminded of the current concern over the military-industrial complex or the cost of the space program to become acutely aware of where the authority for interpreting man's needs presently lies.

The scientist and the technologist are currently presiding over the mysteries of creation and existence. This shift of the "interpretive button" (or the authority to understand and control life) from the hand of the theologian to the scientist is referred to under the general heading of secularization. Nothing dramatizes this more sharply than the comment by President Nixon concerning the landing of the Apollo 11 crew on the moon, "This is the most significant week since the creation of the world." Although this statement may contain some questionable theology, it does capture the mood of a people who are impressed with scientific achievement.

The unreflective churchman may well go on celebrating the achievements of science while he clings to the ingredients of a faith which has seemingly stood the test of time. However, if he is curious enough to push to the bottom of the contemporary situation, he will discover that he must wrestle with the changing times before he can rest assured in the faith.

What happened? What happened to the secure world in which theology and the church once stood so proudly? The church which once claimed to have things under control now finds herself at the bottom of Humpty Dumpty's wall trying to piece together the shattered standards of achievement and authority which stood her in good stead for so long.

Who pushed Humpty Dumpty off of the wall? What has wrenched the rug out from under the church's understanding of her faith and her world? If a process of change has been set in motion which is bent on the total secularization of contemporary attitudes and behavior, then as disciples of the faith we have a job on our hands. Add the seemingly insurmountable task of speaking meaningfully of God to a mentality schooled in an empirical and pragmatic way of life and we have the makings of a major challenge for the life of the church in our day.

There have been many Sir Galahads who have done battle with this issue. The secular discussion has been a preoccupation among theologians during recent years. The debate has been heady and exciting stuff for many a young theologue; although responses to its challenges are by no means limited to the younger set. If we are to pose any valuable alternatives for theology and for the church of the seventies, we must come to grips with the discussions which have surrounded the secularization issue as well as develop an understanding of the deeper causes for that discussion. My task shall be, first of all, to clarify some of the confusion which surrounds the secular terminology and its use by various and sundry individuals. When we discover, for example, that such diverse aspects of life as the complexities of the modern metropolis *and* the mentality of the modern man are said to be secular, then we need to do some critical analysis of the language being used to interpret this phenomenon. We must also set ourselves to the bringing of some semblance of meaning and understanding to the variety of depictions or stances which have been taken toward the process of secularization. Are there in fact several different and distinct types of responses which churchmen are making to the changes and challenges of our day? If we can bring some semblance of order to the discussions, we shall have come a long way in the right direction.

The need for clarity has been laid upon us as well by the flagrant use of such terms as "secular," "secularity," and "secularization"; words which jump out at us from the most unexpected of places in the reading of recent theological journals and books. The abundance of these currently "in" words in contemporary writing and theological thought indicates not only an interest in this area but the definite need for clarification and definition. As Larry Shiner has remarked, "Few catchwords of current theological discussion are sounded with more pathos or are more in need of definition than 'secularization.' " [1]

The use of the term "secular" must be seen within its historical setting. The first meaning which this word usually reflects is the temporal, as opposed to the eternal, stemming from the original meaning of the Latin word *saeculum* — "generation" or "age." In the thought of St. Augustine, *saeculum* meant "the world." The secular came to mean that which belongs to this life, to the here and now, to what is going on in this world. We could also say that the secular has come to mean the this-worldly, as opposed to the creedal affirmations concerning the life of the world to come.

In Christian thought the interpretation of *saeculum* gradually emerged to mean the world as opposed to the church. But confusion surrounding the use of the word increased when distinctions were made within the priestly function itself. The "secular" priests were those who did not live under the discipline of a religious order. Thus we find the need for sorting out the meanings of the language used in this secular talk.

In addition to the difficulty involved in the secular language game, we are confronted with the more crucial question of the legitimacy of speaking of the "process of secularization" as such. Sociologists, historians, and theologians are aware that the complex changes which have occurred in the Western world over the last several centuries have challenged traditional thought patterns, social forms, and patterns of behavior. Some theorists refer to this change under the sweeping category of secularization; others are more reluctant to give it a single designation.

Any theologian or churchman who is currently dealing with this phenomenon is haunted by the question of what is taking place in our society. Is there a dynamic which is operating to create a culture and society which is more "secular" than was the case in other periods of history such as that of tribal Israel, medieval Christendom, or eighteenth-century Europe?

The manner in which much of the discussion about the process of secularization has been carried on presupposes a distinction between the sacred and the secular. If our thinking has been informed by such a distinction, then we must show how the status of the sacred realm is being affected by secular forces. In its faith and practice the church has too often reflected the Pauline doctrine of the separation of the flesh and the spirit. According to Paul, man lived on two planes, the material and the spiritual. Paul would have been horrified to discover that some in the church came to believe in "the resurrection of the flesh"! Whether or not a direct cause-and-effect relationship can be established between the thinking of Paul and contemporary churchmanship, the uneasiness expressed about the possibility of our society becoming more worldly is strikingly similar to the Pauline emphasis upon the strict separation of the flesh and the spirit. Paul's distorted understanding of the relationship between the spirit and the flesh does not help those today for whom the relationship between the church and the world is a problem child. It is the purpose of this discussion to promote an alternative means by which the problem of secularization can be evaluated.

In the material which has come out concerning the sacred-secular debate it seems obvious that there were certain distinct characteristics which divide the various critics into at least four distinct positions. These four perspectives have been designated as follows: "The Sacred Against the Secular," "The Sacred-Secular Paradox," "The Eclipse of the Secular," and "The Death of the Sacred." We shall try to discover the unique contributions of each of these modes of thought as they wrestle with the meaning of "the secular," "secularity," "the process of secularization," and "the relationship between religion and Christianity." Although some of the writers will not fit neatly within the categories provided, nevertheless, this framework will provide a means of systematizing a confusing and divergent body of material. We shall conclude with an attempt to find "The Sacred Through the Secular." (These categories and modes of thought have been put in schematic form in the chart at the back of this book.)

As we travel through the various thought worlds of these writers we shall look carefully at those positions which presuppose the split between the sacred and the secular or between the church and the world. We may discover that there are alternatives to this split-level theology which may enable us to move beyond the sacred-secular impasse. We are hindered in comfortably adopting this split-level thinking by the mood of our times. The current tendency is to polarize when differences are exposed and tensions mount. This defensiveness has for too long characterized the relationship of the church and the world. On the other hand, the lack of a real theological alternative has led some to assume that the sacred and the secular are really not such strange bedfellows, so that we hear of secular churches, secular congregations, secular faith, and secular Christianity. Neither one of these alternatives provides us with the best means of getting at the relationship between the sacred and the secular, or the church and the world.

In a very real sense the task of theology is to carry out a mandate which was laid on us by the readable documents of Colin Williams concerning the church's involvement in the world. The church has not really totally risked her faith and her practice in the world. Only as her theology becomes totally open to being shaped by the pluralistic environment of our society will we discover whether the church can minister to a changing world. Those activistic clergy and laity who have been at the front of racial, political, and peace activities must take more seriously the conditioning effect which that involvement has on the church's theological symbols and mission. Such political involvement now calls for a political theology. It calls for a re-creation of an image of the religious man who is sensitive to and is shaped by all of his experiences in the world, be they the so-called "secular" or the so-called "sacred" dimensions. To do theology politically is to see religion as more than a response to the sacred deposits of truth: it is to see religion as the fundamental human response to all that shapes our lives. Could it be that the political arena is the battleground of salvation, the place where the meaning of human existence must be fought out today?

Such a willingness to do battle in the political area not only challenges the resources of the church's faith, but it also challenges the church's ability to be sensitive to the needs of the world. This understanding of the faith does not allow the church to bring the answers and solutions to the world's problems like a liberal social worker in a deteriorating community. In doing theology politically the church helps the world to "get itself together."

This stance of the church does not allow the man of faith to divide his decisions into those which are sacred and those which are secular. It calls upon the man of faith to draw upon all sources of truth and all levels of experience in order to be a religious man. Such a man of faith is anything but parochial. He is a world citizen. He is called upon to approach life with tools of understanding drawn from a world view grounded in history, shaped by a total awareness of the world situation, and pulled toward a more human future. This kind of openness to the world is what is meant by the phrase "man of faith." For it takes faith to risk oneself openly with other persons. It takes faith to risk our grasp of truth in the public arena. It takes faith to be open to the shaping of all of life and that basis of life which we call God. It takes faith to allow ourselves to challenge the church to be the church.

We hope that our wrestling with the changing times will provide us with a better grasp of what future there is for the clergyman who is sensitive to the times. Our discussion will call the contemporary clergyman to forsake his role as custodian of the church's traditions in order to become a builder of human communities and a theological interpreter of the times. Our discussion will find us revising much of our theological stance and creating the kinds of images and symbols which call forth the best in the human spirit. Whether the institutional church can stand more patches on her cloth is yet to be seen. There may need to be some new garments sewn, and some new wineskins purchased to hold the new wines which are the vintage of our generation.

Change is confronting us. Whether we have the resources of faith to match the challenges of the times is yet to be seen. In a real sense we can find a depth of truth in the simple rhyme, "Love it or leave it, change it or lose it!" When we apply this adage to our concern for the church and her traditions, as well as our sensitivity to the times, we are called to love the church as well as change her so that she might indeed be present to the world. If in being present the church can better enable the world to celebrate life, then we may also discover a mission for the church in the future.

2
The
Sacred
Against
the Secular

The stance which we have designated as "The Sacred Against the Secular" is probably one of the most familiar to us. It has been present since the inception of the life of the church. As one looks at the world through the eyes of the New Testament, one can get the impression that there are several ways of looking at the relationship of the secular (or the world) to the sacred. There was, however, in the world of the New Testament a strong belief that the world and history could no longer be trusted. "This world" or "this age," could not finally support life. Real living must be postponed until "this time" and "this world" were replaced by God's world. This future world would be brought in by cataclysmic forces. Thus we find that Jesus as well as the early Christians had an understanding of the world that was derived from a period of history which had lost confidence in history. This particular understanding of history is known as apocalypticism.

This historical problem became a thorn in the side of the early church. It was the apostle Paul's peculiar problem. His early writings reflect the urgency and impending nature of God's coming rule. Paul urges his adherents to forsake all and to prepare for God's kingdom. If this stance meant holding off on one's marriage until the kingdom was brought in, then one should do so. As time passed, however, Paul began to realize that he might well die of old age rather than witness the end of the age. He thus began to take more seriously the continued survival of the church.

As one looks at the total impression of Paul's writings, one gains an awareness that the apocalyptic cynicism was wearing off and that the early church needed to build a stable institutional base. Whether or not Jesus' hopes for the kingdom of God were justly realized in the established church is now an academic matter. Nevertheless, there have been those who throughout history have claimed that the church was still a pilgrim people and that this world was for the sole purpose of "passing through"!

There is a shop on Chicago's northwest side which sells amulets, herbs, statuary, perfumes, candles, and dolls for the purpose of bringing good luck to their purchasers. One of the potions is called "Desenvolvimiento," which, very loosely, means: "Get me out of this situation." It is purchased by those who wish to have their luck change for the better. It is symbolic of the attitude of those in the "Sacred Against the Secular" category. They are persons who see the Christian faith as a "potion" which will get them out of the present world situation and deliver them to a far better place. Let us look at the world or the secular through the eyes of these persons to see why they feel the secular is to be avoided.

THE SECULAR

The "Sacred Against the Secular" stance in our typology defines the secular as an age very much like the New Testament concept of aeon. It is the present time between the times when men are pilgrims and sojourners in the terrestrial city. Since the world is secular by definition, it is a threat to the religious community which is tempted to take on the color of its surroundings. Persons who hold to this view are less concerned with apologetics to men who have lost their religious sensitivity than with a protest against the triumph of the "world" in the church and a prophetic call to repent and return to the authentic origins of the faith.

This protest against the "things of the world" has taken various forms in the history of Christianity. In the eyes of Troeltsch this stance by a community of people is the "sect-type." That is, it is concerned to withdraw from the secular threat of the world into an enclave or closed community. Frequently such persons have not only set themselves physically apart from the world but theologically as well. This attitude is clearly seen in the Anabaptist movement of the Radical Reformation as well as in such communities as the Amish in contemporary America. These persons seek to escape the threat of worldly institutions. This retreat not only carries with it a basic distrust of the world and history, but it also implies that the world is not God's locus of revelation.

The most adamant of the theological separatists include the evangelistic thrusts of the last century which continue to exert a major influence upon American religious and civic life today. One dominant surge of evangelical pietism began in nineteenth-century Germany in reaction against the scholastic Lutheranism of the time. Pietism, in its assertion of the primacy of feeling in Christian experience, was a radical departure from the scholastic Lutheranism which assumed a fixed, dogmatic interpretation and a rigid, intellectual conformity. Along with this pietism developed an ascetic attitude toward the world.

The kind of pietism known in Germany had a strong similarity to the Wesleyan movement in England. John Wesley was also reacting against the stiff religiosity of the Anglican church. The Wesleyan movement centered in the recovery of Bible reading, the organization of prayer cells, the reform of liturgy and worship, personal piety, and the accent on personal vices and virtues. These evangelicals in England offered people a hope of heaven, a defined place in life, a motive for aspiration, and an outlet for emotional and spiritual energies.

The Wesleyan-Methodist-Pietist-Evangelical experience became a very creative interlude in the history of the church. Its importance for the American religious scene cannot be minimized. The evangelical genius of men such as John Wesley has been profoundly influential upon the contemporary American religious scene. The efforts of Wesley and his followers were directed toward the rural and village areas where people were confronted with the beginnings of the Industrial Revolution. Methodism offered an all-embracing vision of life which fused eternal with temporal concerns.

This brief look at the evangelical and Methodist traditions provides us with clues for understanding the influence which these movements have had on the American scene. The shaping influence which the evangelical distrust of history has had upon the persons who hold the "Sacred Against the Secular" is all too obvious. There is the ever-present concern to keep the faith uncontaminated from dangerous ideas and forces in the culture.

Using the Bible to justify its position, this faith stance desires to preserve the pure tradition in its cloistered fellowship. Like the Amish it sets itself off from the world theologically if not physically as well. This theological separation is accomplished through the use of a clearly defined set of doctrines or beliefs. In order to prevent contamination from the "liberals" or "ecumenicals," persons in fundamentalism mark themselves off from the more progressive theology of the major Protestant bodies in America. They define anyone who does not hold to the following beliefs as worldly or a modernist: 1) the inerrancy of Scripture; 2) the deity of Christ; 3) Christ's virgin birth (understood literally and physically); 4) the substitutionary theory of the atonement (often called "the blood atonement"); and 5) the physical and literal resurrection of Christ. These doctrines are used like a "loyalty oath"! Thus, a fundamentalist is very threatened by worldly Christians who differ in belief.

The difficulty in communicating with this "fundamentalist approach" lies in a basic difference in approaching the scriptural record. We mentioned above, for example, that if one took literally the understanding of Jesus and Paul concerning the apocalyptic end of the age, then one is left with a basic contradiction within the Bible itself.

The most recent attempt in the American scene to call people *out* of the world was the so-called religious revival of the 1950's. This revival was characterized by two distinct emphases. One was the practice of speaking of God anthropomorphically and sentimentally. The other emphasis was the use of a religious language which expressed an immature and almost selfish understanding of the self and its relationship to other selves, the world, and God. This "privatizing" of the faith or salvation is most disastrous.

The failure of American Protestant fundamentalism to develop an affirmative world view is most enlightening for our purposes. Just as it views its theological doctrines as a means of separating the sheep from the goats, so it carries this same negativism into its total understanding of itself in relation to the world. Fundamentalism draws its distinctiveness from its attempt to maintain status by negation.

This reactionary outlook concerning the modern world, but particularly directed toward the "modernistic" churches, seems to be embodied most concretely in the person of Carl McIntire. This spokesman for the "Far Right" in the church has spent over thirty-five years spreading disruption and dissent among clergy and laity. No problem has arisen in any Protestant body that he has not sought to exploit in his fight against "modernist" churches that belong to such "demonic" structures as the National Council of Churches. McIntire has repeatedly attempted to confuse the public and the press by holding conferences of his own groups in the same locations and at the same times as meetings of the National Council of Churches or the World Council of Churches are being held.

Most recently Dr. McIntire has "reacted to" the Black Manifesto of James Forman by proposing a manifesto of the International Council of Christian Churches. He has claimed that the "modernist" churches are morally obliged to pay reparations to the true church; namely, those associated with the International Council of Christian Churches, which he founded some years ago. The self-righteousness of a Carl McIntire should not prevent us from seeing the agenda (hidden or otherwise) which he brings. Although they claim to speak the loudest against the church's becoming tainted by the world, quite possibly he and others of a similar persuasion present the clearest portrayal of an attempt to establish one kind of kingdom of God on earth.

> The kind of reformation desired by right-wing Christians is fairly clear. It is the subjugation of all serious thought to an unimaginative fundamentalism and the implementation of a social counter-

revolution that would bring the middle-class elements of the South and Midwest into power in America.[1]

The "Sacred Against the Secular" has other adherents of a more moderate position as well. Although their statements may not be of the reactionary order of a Carl McIntire, they still maintain a stance of condescension toward the world or the secular. This attitude is typified in the following remark by Micklem: "The latter [sacred] has no meaning except in relation to the secular, and its very purpose is to redeem and consecrate the secular."[2] The secular in this perspective includes all human activities and institutions concerned with the world, and which are products of man's creative capacity. On the other hand, the sacred is that which has or claims to have about it a transcendent quality: absoluteness of value or a quality of the unconditional and the final. Although the portrayal is not in reactionary or negative tones; nevertheless, the secular does come in for second-class citizenship.

Similarly Itty contends that the secular is dependent upon the spiritual realm for its existence. Only a spiritually based inclusive cause can bring about personal wholeness and integrate the various worlds or spheres which compete for man's loyalty.

> The spiritual basis is not intended to absolutize and invoke religious sanction for social structures, but rather to preserve their genuine secular character, their historical provisional, relative, functional, and experimental nature, and at the same time permeating them with spiritual values.[3]

Although it is obvious that men like Micklem and Itty maintain the superior status of the sacred, they at least are wrestling with the issues of the world in contrast to those whose only concern is purifying the "worldly church."

Blamires carries the fear which McIntire expresses for the church into the arena of the individual's confrontation with the world. Blamires is concerned to preserve what he calls the "Christian mind" in the midst of the competing pluralities of life.

> Christian personalities are being truncated and deformed by the fact that men and women have to leap about from one tradition of discourse to another as they move in thought and discussion from moral matters to political matters, from ecclesiastical matters to cultural matters.[4]

Although Blamires is definitely wrestling with the right issues, he has not been able to bring them into a comprehensive enough schema for critical examination. His failure is that of this entire "Sacred Against the Secular" stance. It is not historical enough! In distinction from other adherents to this stance, at least Micklem, Itty, and Blamires are sufficiently aware of history to feel the threat of the changing times and to have the awareness that this means something to the church. However, the basic weakness of this stance is that it does not allow history and the secular world to enliven and widen its experience of faith. Even so, this kind of faith is never at a loss for words. It can go on talking with extraordinary superiority about God and the world. But it lacks urgency and the taste of reality.

From these remarks we can begin to capture not only the thinking of those within the "Sacred Against the Secular," but also to gain clues about the style of ministry which would be the outgrowth of such thinking. For example, the churches which adhere to the proclamations of a Carl McIntire will set forth a definite style of ministry. Their reactions to the racial crisis, foreign relations, interchurch dialogue, and a genuine openness to the world are almost predictable.

The dominant thrust of this stance is that the church is responsible for the preservation of the deposit of faith (the sacred) in the face of the threat of secularizing processes inherent in the various institutions and attitudes found in the world. In this style of ministry the Christian is responsible to bring to the secular arena the "saving" qualities of sacred realities for which the church is the custodian. For adherents of this stance the secular is a hostile world.

SECULARITY

"Secularity" is the coined word which stands for a frame of mind or particular mentality which one thinks is predominant in the present world. A particular style of thinking is designated as secular if it supplants the older concepts of ultimate meaning in a culture undergoing secularization. Contemporary man's way of thinking includes his attitudes, preferences, and convictions. This mentality must be checked against the mentality of other generations and other ages to see if a definite mutation has taken place which designates contemporary man as secular.

An individual who has expended great efforts to point up the relative nature of the world view of the Judaeo-Christian tradition has been Rudolf Bultmann. He has seen the importance of recognizing that man's views of the world need to be continually revised in order to cope with the changing times. He maintained that there was a definite connection between "the times" and the mentality used to cope with that world. Bultmann's efforts were focused upon freeing the message of the New Testament from the outdated wrappings of the first-century mentality in order that it might be allowed to travel in the orbit of twentieth-century thinking.

The challenge which Bultmann laid on the church must be picked up regardless of one's peculiar stance. Whether one considers the treasures of history to be museum pieces or living things of faith depends upon the position which he takes in regard to the Christian faith.

If the secular stands for a hostile world, then secularity or the mentality of that world is also a threat to those who maintain the "Sacred Against the Secular"! As we noted above, possibly the dominant thrust of this stance is the evangelistic tradition. It has fought valiantly to save men out of the world. Its camp meetings, revivals, classes, and congregations have been geared toward rescuing solitary individuals from the hostile world. The individual thus saved out of the world considered himself to have been chosen by Jesus, his personal savior. The evangelical revivals and crusades have always held forth the "body count," that is, the number of conversions recorded, and such churches always make a great deal of their membership gains and losses.

The striving on the part of the new evangelicals to revitalize the nineteenth-century interpretation of Protestant orthodoxy is best seen in the work of evangelists such as Billy Graham, and the publication efforts of *Christianity Today*. They have been involved in a sustained effort to bring about a reformation in the Protestant churches of America — a return to the evangelical theology of the past century. The witticism that changes the name of *Christianity Today* to "Christianity Yesterday" is not without a point. There is an inherent longing in this tradition to return to essentially nineteenth-century elements of the church and American culture.

The increasing gap in understanding between the new evangelical or conservative and much of what is going on in American culture is due in part to the way in which words are being created and used as symbols. The struggle to reformulate traditional symbols and create new meanings can be confusing and threatening, so much so that some wonder what is happening. What is happening within and without the church is the great "conspiracy" of the sensitive who create symbols and do not take them literally, while the insensitive react in horror to symbols such as "the death of God" and "turning on, tuning in, and dropping out." The failure of the new evangelical to speak to the sophisticated culture of our day is proven by the fact that the evangelical continues to use his words and symbols in a more or less literal way and accepts the words and symbols of others in the same unsophisticated sense.

The most famous contemporary exponent of the "Sacred Against the Secular" stance is Billy Graham. He not only portrays extremely well the theological underpinnings of this stance, but he has also more recently come to identify himself with the popular religiosity of the Nixon Administration. For example, Mr. Graham quoted with approval the President's inaugural sentiment that "all our problems are spiritual and must, therefore, have a spiritual solution." The Nixon-Graham doctrine of the relation of religion to public morality and policy was made even more visible by the presence of Mr. Graham at the White House worship service shortly after it was initiated.

The danger inherent in this stance, as demonstrated in the style of Billy Graham, is that it seems indifferent to the distinction which should be made between conventional religion and radical religious protest. Conventional religion of the Billy Graham variety is too frequently content to throw an aura of sanctity on contemporary public policy even if that policy is morally inferior or even outrageously unjust. Radical religious protest, on the other hand, subjects all historical reality (including economic, social, and radical injustice) to the "word of the Lord," i.e., absolute standards of justice. We must painfully ask ourselves the question: Why is it that the Billy Graham who preaches most strongly the offense of the cross is so *inoffensive?*

The Nixon-Graham doctrine also assumes that a religious change of heart, such as occurs in an individual conversion, would cure men of all sin. Billy Graham has a favorite text: "If any man be in Christ, he is a new creature." Graham applies this Pauline hope about conversion to the racial problem, for example, as he assures that "if you live in Christ, you become color-blind." The defect of this confidence in individual conversion is that it obscures the fact that individuals are also social beings. In fact we may even be social selves first and only individuals secondarily. At the least we cannot minimize the need for examining the individual as well as the social character of our virtues and vices.[5]

We previously cited Blamires as representing a more moderate and possibly more sane approach within the "Sacred Against the Secular" stance. With regard to secularity Blamires sees the purity of the "Christian mind" being eroded by the relativities of secularism:

> There is no longer a Christian mind.
> It is a commonplace that the mind of modern man has been secularized. For instance, it has been deprived of any orientation towards the supernatural. . . . As a *thinking* being, the modern Christian has succumbed to secularization.[6]

Blamires is convinced that there is a manner of thinking which is peculiar to the Christian. In fact, he claims that a Christian uses different mental categories to assess the world from those of a man who is unschooled in the thought forms of Christianity. Blamires makes the claim that contemporary men may think pragmatically or politically, but not Christianly.

If Blamires' thought were not so dependent upon a supernatural orientation, we might find it more palatable. The "supernatural ace" which he keeps up his sleeve is not only difficult to appreciate but it is a most severe stumbling block for many. Almost before the ink on such words has been allowed to dry, one can hear our evangelical friends off in the wings whispering loudly, "The gospel is always foolishness to the Greeks!" It would appear that a careful examination of just this point would bear much fruit when it comes to sorting out the challenges of contemporary ways of thinking without a supernatural understanding of God — the challenges of secularity.

From the perspective of the "Sacred Against the Secular," secularity becomes the attitude or mind-set which evaluates its world apart from a supernatural bearing or understanding. Secularity is thus like a radioactive cloud hanging over the heads of those who maintain the Christian faith as basically oriented toward a supernatural realm. A person who maintains such a Christian mentality is living in two worlds. On Sunday he responds Christianly while during the week he responds politically, economically, or socially depending upon the context and situation. A person of this persuasion is involved in two ball games while he is keeping only one scorecard. The game which he plays in the world does not affect his standing with the "Big League." Only those games played according to supernatural rules will get him into the World Series of eternal life. Again we can only say that while such an unhistorical ball game may not be sane, it is safe!

THE PROCESS OF SECULARIZATION

Is there something happening in our world which is making American culture more secular? Has the development of the city invalidated the basically rural orientation of the evangelical faith? Will technology actually make such a faith obsolete? The way these questions have been put could most likely cause a person of evangelical persuasion to become as nervous as a Christian Scientist with appendicitis! Nevertheless, the issues cannot be avoided by the evangelical or by any man of faith.

The development of the city and increased industrial activity had a profound effect upon the American evangelical empire. The increased development of a genuine religious pluralism in America challenged the vise-like grip which conservative Protestantism has held. The conflict of value systems which has been found to be increasingly present in our cities since the middle of the nineteenth century has had a profound effect upon what was previously an overwhelming control of American religious life by evangelicals. Add to this the scientific and inventive preoccupations of the contemporary industrial-technological society and one has the makings for a first-rate religious mental breakdown.

The impending identity crisis was there for all to see in a society which associated spirituality with rural values. As society moved toward pluralism the American evangelical empire began to crack. After all, was not this society greatly influenced by the injection of pietistic-individualistic values held so dear by the evangelical world? The recognition of the nature of this threat provides us with an understanding of why the evangelicals make up the predominant thrust in the "Sacred Against the Secular" household.

The last century of American history provides us with the clues for understanding the evangelical identity crisis. The evangelical empire was built on the same "manifest destiny" dream which brought the good life to many an enterprising person. The belief was commonly shared if not self-consciously articulated that God had indeed given his own people the continent to be possessed and subdued. The self-made man became the new ideal in America in contrast to the old European aristocrat or the earlier American man content with his station in life.

The self-made man "kept hearing the minister invoking the old language of heaven and hell, rewards and punishment. But on the temporal side of that transcendent curtain, all was different. The message was not, 'Be contented!' but 'Get ahead!' " [7] Such use and abuse of the evangelical initiative posed a new challenge for the evangelical tradition of the mid-nineteenth century. How was one to account for the successful evangelical? The custodians of the soul were now being called upon to enable people to rise in their calling and not out of it.

These newly-rich at first seemed to want the benefit of clergy for their passage. They had not inherited blood or land, but they had been successful traders, speculators, and merchants. The Puritan had been told to be suspicious of the rich. The evangelical had been told to be content if he was not rich. The American in the mid-nineteenth century was beginning to be told to get rich.[7]

The willingness to pronounce the "amen" for individual achievement as long as such achievement doesn't challenge the sacred cows of personal morality is still clinging like a pious monkey to the back of popular American religiosity — it's all right to take advantage of a man in the capitalistic system as long as you don't sleep with his wife!

This evangelical schizophrenia was exposed by the developing urban scene of the late nineteenth century. For the evangelical the city became the root of the industrial problem. Just as the locomotive interrupted the pastoral beauty of the prairie, two millenniums of pastoral imagery from the Bible which had nurtured the spirituality of Western culture were being challenged as well. The evangelicals of the nineteenth century were faced with the same theological question which is severely testing the contemporary American Protestant church; namely, is it possible to develop an urban spirituality? Is it possible to translate the simplicity, innocence, fresh opportunity, and unclaimed destiny of American frontier life into the creative possibilities of urban life?

The evangelicals of the last century agreed with many of their contemporaries outside the church that to look back to history and to Europe was to look back to a complexity and an urban life for which none of them cared. The gospel primitivism which sustained them in the transition to the new world was totally inadequate for the demands of the contemporary industrial-urban age. Hence, this strategic decision to walk backwards into the future has left the evangelical without a positive contribution to the discussion of secularization. The process of secularization has been resisted because it threatens the secure religious empire of the past century. Thus the sacred stands once more *against* the secular!

The process of secularization is a very real threat to those within the "Sacred Against the Secular" position. The withdrawal of areas of life and activity from the control of organized religious bodies, and the withdrawal of areas of thought from the control of what are believed to be religious truths seem demonic from this perspective. This position continues to maintain that the Spirit has manifested himself in a saving or transcending way only in the events recorded in the Bible and most specifically in the events of Jesus' life, death, and resurrection. Any challenge to this authority cannot be tolerated.

Because few persons in this perspective have really taken the challenges of secularization seriously, we find it difficult to refer to a critically reflective position taken by any such adherents. However, Lesslie Newbigin, from his more moderate position, has wrestled with the awareness of the increasing assertion of the competence of human science and techniques to handle human problems of every kind. The church no longer has a corner on humanitarianism, for example. The Great Physician no longer hangs his shingle on the church door. The great thinkers are no longer primarily the products of the religious or theological centers.

Newbigin almost moves himself out of the "Sacred Against the Secular" camp by admitting that the roots of modern science and technology may well lie within the biblical understanding of man and nature. The process of secularization may have a real continuity with the biblical-prophetic history insofar as it rests upon the freedom of man to exercise a delegated authority over the natural world without fear of any "powers" other than the Creator himself; insofar as it seeks the freedom, dignity, and welfare of man as man, and it challenges all authorities which deny this common human dignity; insofar as it brings all mankind to a recognition of the interdependence of all life. Newbigin concludes that the "restless dynamism" which has created and sustained the process of secularization is fed from the biblical faith in a meaningful history.[8]

At two distinct points we are stretching the case to include Newbigin in this schema. First of all, his claim that the Judaeo-Christian tradition is a primary ingredient in the process of secularization would be more than a horror story to most persons in the "Sacred Against the Secular" position. Secondly, his affirmation of history as the location of God's activity places him distinctly in opposition to those who hold a warped apocalyptic understanding of contemporary history. To such persons the only history worthy of God's activity was biblical history. Since then the water, land, and sky have been too "polluted" for *His* presence! The point at which Newbigin fits into the "Sacred Against Secular" pattern is in his claim that God in his grace (and, by implication, the church and its resources) provides the most meaningful answers to the problems of history and culture. Newbigin is concerned to maintain the primary influence of the Judaeo-Christian tradition.

An individual who has not only taken the scientific-technological world with utmost seriousness but who would take exception with those such as Newbigin who might claim that the Judaeo-Christian tradition provided the creative ingredients for that world is Jacques Ellul. Ellul has addressed himself to the technological phenomenon and the threat which it poses for modern man. In his book *The Technological Society* Ellul depicts what he considers to be the tendency of a technological society to determine man's life against his will. The essential tragedy of the Western civilization is that it is becoming increasingly dominated by what Ellul calls "technique." Technical activity automatically eliminates every spontaneous activity or transforms it into technical activity. "There is no place for an individual today unless he is a technician." [9]

Ellul maintains that "technique" has achieved a sufficient autonomy from economic or political control and moral or spiritual judgment so that man is no longer in control of his destiny. Man's social fabric is being destroyed and the mutated result is a desacralized collection of individuals. "More than science which limits itself to explaining the 'how,' 'technique' desacralizes because it demonstrates that mystery does not exist." [10]   Science exposes what was previously held to be sacred, "technique" takes possession of it and enslaves it. Man feels himself responsible for his own destiny, but is not. He does not feel himself an object of the technological order, but he is. He has become *homo economicus!*

If Ellul would agree that the Judaeo-Christian tradition were a primary factor in the development of the scientific-technological society, he would surely claim that its offspring is a bastard child at best. Science and technology have taken over the creative process and are creating a world in other than God's own image! The uneasiness of those in Ellul's position comes from their belief that preoccupation with scientific and technological achievement may very likely undermine the moral fabric and the critical judgments of a society. There is a very real fear that science has become modern man's sacred cow. The vitamin so frequently replaces the crucifix. Even Saint Christopher is not safe from the threat of modernity!

However, some hopeful signs indicate that concerned scientists and technologists are open to theological and ethical input. That is, they are aware that they are dealing with the "mysteries" of the universe and are gravely concerned with the far-reaching implications of their research and discoveries. Their success just emphasizes the need for the church and the man of faith to deal with the agenda which science and technology have laid at the doorstep of modern man. Whether man has sold his birthright as a free and creative being for the thrill of scientific discovery is not yet clear.

Whether or not one agrees with the stance which Ellul has taken toward the contemporary world, one must commend his pioneering efforts. In a very systematic way he has set forth the effects of the contemporary world upon the life of man. He has correctly recognized that the technological order sets many of the boundaries within which creative change and redirection of our society can take place. Whether or not man is a slave to his creation is not presently discernible.

The important role which the Christian community should play in the ever-present technological society cannot be minimized. The church contains the potential resources which can help "save" individual responsibility and protect man from being stripped of meaning by the technological conditions of contemporary industrial society. Whether or not those within the "Sacred Against the Secular" stance are best equipped to deal with this challenge is highly debatable. However, the evangelical tradition has not been very effective at the point where the industrial-technological age has intersected with the contemporary American society; namely, in the heart of urban America.

The evangelical tradition with its predominantly rural mentality has been able to sustain itself in rural America and gain a strong inroad into suburbia by means of sanctioning the morality and piety of the suburbanite. However, the evangelical tradition with its accent upon individual behavior has not even begun to deal effectively with the problems which technological development is causing in America. The question is no longer one of saving man out of his dire condition. Either we begin "saving" the total human condition with its scientific-technological implications or we will save nothing!

Evangelical Christianity is attempting to reformulate the symbols and doctrines of faith to which Americans have instinctively gravitated. There has, however, been a real resistance to attempts made to adapt the gospel to the needs of modern man. This hesitation is especially noticeable with reference to attitudes taken toward the ecumenical movement or the social involvement of clergymen and churches. One senses in the evangelical response a concern for the causes of human oppression and need, but also the lack of theological understanding as to how one shares the vision of faith with a world in need. This ambiguity within the evangelical position was most clearly exposed in the "Penultimate" column which appeared in *The Christian Century:*

> Evangelist Billy Graham was interviewed recently in San Francisco. With indomitable courage, Graham spoke out on several controversial issues:
>
> On capital punishment: "I take no position."
>
> On therapeutic abortion: "That's a complicated question, I'm not going to get involved."
>
> On whether he approves of a bill to restrict the teaching of evolution in California public schools: "I'd have to see the bill."
>
> On whether the Southern Baptist Convention should join the National Council of Churches: "I'll leave that to the Southern Baptists."
>
> [On] the real problem in America today . . . : the nation's leaders are "not meeting [youth's] moral needs." [11]

Behind the humor of the column there is a critical indictment of the evangelical tradition which finds itself in a sophisticated society without the theological tools to deal with that society. Where is the evangelistic fervor which propelled that tradition into "prime time" in the American religious scene! The reticence of Mr. Graham's remarks seem more akin to a campaigning politician trying to avoid risk issues than a man of faith facing courageously a contemporary world needing to be humanized.

Exposed in the above is the glaring American popular religious assumption that a preacher may very well criticize a public official for crawling into bed with someone else's wife, but he is not to protest if that official's policies enslave or brutalize people. The attractiveness of this arrangement to social, economic, and political leaders is obvious. It permits complete autonomy and uncritical development of their approach as long as they keep their personal morality pure. Nevertheless, when the politician steps on the church's toes — elimination of prayers from the public schools, legalized gambling — then those in the evangelical tradition can talk politics and receive a popular response.[12] Evangelicalism has made itself particularly attractive to those who have the greatest stake in the status quo. This assertion is not to deny that there are self-sacrificial evangelicals in the inner city involved in humanitarian and benevolent activities. Nor can we contend that it is not possible for private evangelicals to lead wholly private lives, hoping in God and believing in Jesus Christ, apart from the world. However, whenever evangelicalism takes on a partisan character, whenever it rallies and organizes and mobilizes as a social force, it is willy-nilly involved in the political realm as a churchly form and movement.

An example of what is being said is clearly seen in the activities of the Rev. Paul D. Lindstrom, a member of the John Birch Society, who has drawn national attention through his intercessory role in relation to the Pueblo crew which was hijacked by the North Korean Government. As leader of the "Remember the Pueblo Committee" he played an active role in negotiating between persons within North Korea and our own State Department concerning information about the crew and their eventual release. Since that time his energies have been similarly directed toward prisoners of war in North Vietnam. His style illustrates the ambiguity of those who maintain that the church should not be involved in the political scene and yet find themselves most directly involved in that scene.

The evangelical or conservative tradition is particularly exploitable by a nationalist, military, industrial, and business elite and ordinarily speaks predictably for the point of view associated with civic and societal religions. This generalization is clearly borne out by the activities and pronouncements of a Carl McIntire or a Paul Lindstrom. Can this allegiance of interests still allow the Christian faith to represent the prophets and Jesus against the religion of the pious, against the faithlessness of the people? Can the evangelical tradition represent the stable center of gravity in society, the taken-for-granted solid base, and still shatter the powers that be with a thunder of judgment, or redeem the world with a message of healing? Evangelicalism's future contribution to Protestantism, to the church at large, and to the world will depend upon the degree that it can extricate itself from such a wholly predictable identification with one kind of political force.

RELIGION AND CHRISTIANITY

In this final section of the chapter we shall be concerned to discover the attitude which the "Sacred Against the Secular" stance takes toward religion. By religion we shall mean the embodiment of symbols or doctrines of faith in the forms of a given culture. For example, Jesus' assault upon the money changers in the temple was a very dramatic act showing his attitude toward one particular cultural expression as it was found in the temple of his day. The question with which we shall be concerned here is the degree to which the faith of those in the "Sacred Against Secular" stance is acculturated in spite of their verbal and demonstrative claims to the opposite.

Soren Kierkegaard powerfully set forth his concern for a purified church. His well-known *Attack upon Christendom* was driven by the desire to extract the pseudo-religious forms from the church's institutional life and its theological stance. He was deeply troubled by the church's inability to be prophetic because of the mixed loyalties which permeated the cultural religion of his day. The following statement powerfully portrays his indignation concerning the state of affairs in the church which he knew so well:

> And this end has been attained, has been best attained, indeed completely, in Protestantism, especially in Denmark, in the Danish even-tempered jovial mediocrity. When one sees what it is to be a Christian in Denmark, how could it occur to anyone that this is what Jesus Christ talks about: cross and agony and suffering, crucifying the flesh, suffering for the doctrine, being salt, being sacrificed, etc.? No, in Protestantism, especially in Denmark, Christianity marches to a different melody, to the tune of "Merrily we roll along, roll along, roll along" — Christianity is enjoyment of life, tranquillized, as neither the Jew nor the pagan was, by the assurance that the thing about eternity is settled, settled precisely in order that we might find pleasure in enjoying this life, as well as any pagan or Jews.[13]

Kierkegaard's manifesto against acculturated Christianity as he knew it still echoes in our midst. Every sect, every denomination, every local body of believers has developed this sensitivity to some degree. Whether or not they can rightly claim to be God's White Knight against the evil forces of acculturation is debatable.

Kierkegaard vigorously protested against all forms of church religiosity in his day which were unable or unwilling to speak prophetically and redemptively to the developing industrial society. Although many would contend that the "Sacred Against the Secular" adherents fail to hit the mark at which Kierkegaard aimed his arrows, they nevertheless contend to be God's ambassadors or guardians of the purity of the faith. In one thing they are certainly most correct; namely, that adaptation to culture can become the "Achilles' heel" of Christianity.

In spite of the rigor with which the adherents of this stance pursue this issue, one wonders whether they are as free from institutional and cultural stagnation as they claim. The question is not whether one wishes to embody his faith in cultural-religious expressions. The real test is whether he is aware of the cultural baggage which he carries as a man of faith. Those who speak most vehemently against the false religions of the day fail to realize that much of their religious pattern is informed by the religious expressions of a previous generation. The test which Kierkegaard put to the church is still valid; namely, whether or not the church is speaking prophetically and redemptively to the technological-industrial society. Those within the "Sacred Against the Secular" stance most frequently adhere to a nineteenth-century understanding of the world which is just as acculturated as any world view and must be submitted to the same rigors as any truly prophetic faith. Such a self-awareness can bring none other than a critical humility.

These remarks become most illuminating as we look at the areas of life most affected by the evangelical tradition in America. The adherents of this position have enjoyed a popularity and success in recent decades which cannot be easily ignored. The American Civic Religion has called for the high priests of the faith to pronounce the invocations and benedictions at Presidential prayer breakfasts, Inaugural Day proceedings, Little League and garden club festivities, and numerous other symbolic occasions. In the process the American religious scene has been "boxed in." That is, it has accepted the role of addressing itself to the personal, familial, and leisurely sectors of life while the public dimensions — political, social, economic, cultural — have become autonomous or passed under the control of other kinds of tutelage. The presence of a United Methodist Bishop on the platform of the Democratic Convention for the purpose of pronouncing the benediction, for example, only sharpened the absurdity of the "police riot" which was taking place in the streets of Chicago in August, 1968.

Although religious leaders have been allowed to do some monitoring, some inspiring, and some legitimizing of the larger culture, they have also allowed themselves to be satisfied with the privatizing of religion. This process is the peculiar American version of the process of secularization.[14] The American church has for the most part been willing to accept this boxed-in role. The clergy have been encouraged to give their clerical blessing to the missions and purposes of the nation which symbolized the manifest destiny of God, but their challenges to the political, economic, or social system have been widely criticized. In this regard the attitude taken by the evangelicals toward the city is again crucial.

> The clergy tended to welcome technology as part of God's plan for subduing nature and making individuals rich, but they did fear the cities. The cities were gathering places for reformers and radicals, where people of competing value systems could mingle with new immigrants and disrupt the stability and class situation which supported the evangelical empire.[15]

The difficulty of coming to grips with the extent to which the evangelical tradition is caught up in culture religion is illustrated in Marty's paraphrase of a remark of the apostle Paul, "When you ignorantly worship, him I declare unto you" — "Whom you ignorantly worship, him will I kill off, if only I can catch him." [16] The impurities of faith in the "Sacred Against the Secular" stance must be sorted out before we can claim that it speaks with clarity concerning the acculturation of the American church. This stance contains too much of the deposit of all the values that the American people have held dear for decades. The baptism of the values of the white, northern-European-descended Protestant minority of the American people, identifying racial segregation, states' rights, and a rugged individualism as Christian principles, leaves something to be desired.

The real danger in this kind of affirmation of the American way lies in the possibility of the civic religion's turning into a religious nationalism which allows for no heresy and no critical self-examination. An America which is constantly invoking God along with the promulgation of Protestant-type moral values domestically and internationally needs to be viewed with concern. This lack of self-criticism is the major blind spot in the vision of the "Sacred Against the Secular" stance. It, too, swims in the muddy waters of the American cultural scene. Its institutions have been peculiarly shaped by the forces and thrust of our society.

CONCLUDING REMARKS

When the apostle Paul criticized the world and in fact renounced it in Romans 12:2, "Do not be conformed to this world," he was critical not of solidarity with the world but of conformism with it. This fine yet crucial distinction is most often missed by those adherents of the "Sacred Against the Secular" stance. They have seen their peculiar vocation to be that of a corrective agent to what they see as the worldly lethargy which threatens the life of the church. This prophetic concern should be grounded, however, in the Judaeo-Christian awareness that the people of faith are a part of one history and one world. Divorce from this thrust always means risking death like a fish out of water. Persons who have preserved and called forth an isolation from the world have done a grave injustice to the biblical theme of being present to the world's needs and possibilities.

The reduction of the "sacred realm" to the point of seeing God as merely functioning as an ecclesiastical deity who is interested in personal problems, but who is hardly the creator and sustainer of the whole world, is disastrous. Excessive preoccupation with personal salvation and insensitivity toward what is going on around us is using religion as an escape.

As concerned churchmen our challenge is to be aware

that we cannot and must not simply "go on believing" behind locked doors, as though before Pentecost. We must face the crisis of this new world which our scientific-technological society is thrusting upon us. Did not the apostle Paul himself say, "All things are yours, whether . . . the world or life or death or the present or the future, all are yours; and you are Christ's; and Christ is God's" (1 Corinthians 3:21-23)? To belong to Christ is not to betray the world. The price of being a Christian is to accept special responsibility for the world, to be ready to be exposed and given over to it. Ascetic flight from the world should never be accepted as a possibility. Such a flight would only be a deceptive entry into some artificial world beside this one (generally only the more convenient religious world situation of yesterday).

In conclusion let it be said that we do need to recover the sense of apocalyptic concern found so prevalent in the "Sacred Against the Secular" position. But we must not be satisfied to merely recover it. We must demythologize it! That is, we must allow its radical denial of that which is evil and destructive in the present human condition to speak to us. This sense of world denial is the kind which comes to us in the rage of contemporary angry young men who call for the creation of a new order of society. When the church begins to align herself with this kind of distrust of corrupt aspects of her world, then she may receive the kind of trust she deserves from those who are presently alienated from her world as well as from her sanctuary.

3
The
Sacred-
Secular
Paradox

Just as we discovered that there were certain historical roots for the "Sacred Against the Secular" stance, so the same can be said for the participants in the "Sacred-Secular Paradox." The persons who hold to this position are descendants of the dialectical theology of the 1930's. Thus we must come to understand the Barthian school of thought and its presuppositions which permeate this stance before we can come to understand the peculiar affirmation of the secular which is prevalent in the disciples of Barth.

Karl Barth stamped the sacred-secular split quite indelibly upon the theological mentality of the twentieth century. He vehemently opposed all attempts to talk about God, because he considered them to be human fabrications. God was not to be approached by man-on-his-own. It is God who makes the gesture toward man. Likewise, there is nothing in creation which gives man any clues about divine reality. Having posited the utter transcendence of God and the secularity of the created order, Barth set the stage for the celebrators of the secular who have emerged during the last two decades.

Those who have followed the Barthian appeal have called

the decline of Christianity the most significant event within Western civilization. They have tended to see the loss of the awareness of the sacred as not only irreversible but to be celebrated as well. All forms of religiosity are to be stripped from the rudiments of faith. The other side of this coin is that the created order is to be celebrated as truly secular because it contains no absolutes which can claim man's ultimate loyalty.

Although several prominent theologians had been addressing the question of secularization for years, not until Harvey Cox delivered *The Secular City* did the "secular" become a household word! Cox's "secular manifesto" came at a point in history when the mood of the country was ripe for such a word. The optimism of the early sixties was genuinely embodied in the Kennedy years and carried over into the hoped-for Great Society. One was led to believe that the city, indeed the secular city, was to be embraced and celebrated. The faith-filled pragmatism of John F. Kennedy needed only to be theologically affirmed. Harvey Cox did that for us.

We can affirm with Meland that the interest expressed in *The Secular City* was not so much geared to *what* was said, as concerned *that* it was said with such gusto. As Meland related at the time, "What is arresting about Professor Cox's work is the stance he assumes in confronting the new secular age." [1] Let us go and see the things which he (Barth, Cox, and others) hath wrought!

THE SECULAR

The meaning which the secular takes on for Cox reveals the strong Barthian influence:

> Secular man's values have been deconsecrated, shorn of any claim to ultimate or final significance. . . . He must live with the realization that the rules which guide his ethical life will seem just as outmoded to his descendants as some of his ancestors' practices now appear to him. [2]

The two motifs which come through in this remark are that there is nothing in this world which can claim man's ultimate commitment, and, beyond that and by direct implication, man must be ready to swing with change.

This understanding of the secular is shared by and large

by the following members of the "Barthian School": Gogarten, Bonhoeffer, Van Leeuwen, Van Peursen, and Cox. Not only is man to live out his life without any neat metaphysical system which holds things together for him; not only must man live at the crossroads of many competing loyalties and options; but man is called to embrace just such a world because he has been given the responsibility for re-creating and shaping that world.

Who can deny that a child born in this generation has been forced to come to grips with more problems and to be open to more expressions of reality than his parents ever dreamed would be necessary or possible! The "new math" is not the only thing which is new for Junior. He views the world and its many manifestations through electronic contraptions which would have frightened Grandpa. The space age has not only turned the past on its head at many points but it has taught Junior to count "down" as well.

While the adherents to the "Sacred Against the Secular" feel threatened by this change of events, the word from the "Sacred-Secular Paradox" is that man must live fully in this contemporary culture and wrestle with its competing ideals and ideologies. The result is that no institutional (not even the church's) or personal (least of all the Christian's) concepts or patterns of behavior are above the threat or scrutiny of the penetrating process of change.

Those who adhere to the implications of the Barthian paradox (let God be God and the world be secular) affirm that man has been released from idolatrous loyalties to individual cultural expressions by the act of God in Christ. Therefore, no new development can become a threat to one's faith. One is freed in Christ to live responsibly in a "liberated" world. The secular thus becomes in this perspective the total of man's environment, which has been secularized by the redemptive activity of God.

The affirmation of the secular on the part of Cox and others and the resultant reaction to their claims have made the term "secular" to be possibly the most used and abused word in theological literature in the past ten years. We have been called to live a secular faith, attend secular churches, build secular congregations in secular cities, so that our secular Christianity might be vital in this secular age. If there is any person whose theological computer has not been short-circuited by the apparent contradictory terms, then he is one of the more rare individuals to come upon the theological scene in recent years.

Basic to the "Sacred-Secular Paradox" is the theological assumption that anything is quite possibly secular because nothing is sacred except God.

SECULARITY

If the world is truly secular, then what kind of man is it that lives in that world? At the center of the "Sacred-Secular Paradox" position there hangs a picture of the secular man: man as a practical, problem-solving, controlling being who is less and less preoccupied with questions about ultimates and about the meaning of the universe. He is the kind of man who, in Eric Hoffer's words, has recognized that God and the priests have become unimportant and yet the world and life go on as usual. Even beyond that, secular man may have gone beyond the disinterested role to become, in the lineage of Nietzsche, a God-slayer.

Ever since Bonhoeffer heralded the arrival of modern man or the "man come of age," there have been numerous theological-anthropologists attempting to specify and locate such a man. This search for the "historical secular man" has been diligently pursued by Bonhoeffer and his latter-day saints. This so-called secular man not only possesses freedom but he is utterly responsible for a world in which no superior power is available to make things right when man has "botched things up." This secular man is the first person to realize fully what it means to be human because he has discovered that he has such power within his grasp.

This historical quest for the authentic secular man can be traced through the "Sacred-Secular Paradox" people. Their concern for man's freedom and an understanding of man-on-his-own is grounded in a common antipathy toward metaphysics. The contributions of August Comte to the writings of Cox and Van Peursen are quite significant.

Comte's positivism was based on a theory of the history of mental activity divided into three stages: the theological,

the metaphysical, and the positivist or scientific. He interpreted man in history as having matured beyond the use of
theology and metaphysics. Man, according to Comte, has
turned his attention to understanding the world from a rigor-
ously scientific point of view. Comte claimed that it is no
longer possible for man to organize his world around some
metaphysical scheme.

Comte's schema has been baptized by Van Peursen so that
the three contrasting attitudes are described as follows: the
period of myth with its world of enchantment and magic; the
ontological period in which man sought better control of his
world by developing a rational understanding of it; and the
functional period with man's increasing confidence in his
ability to understand and control the forces of life and the
world with the aid of pragmatic initiative and scientific inquiry.[3]

According to Van Peursen, the mythical stage of primitive
society found man "at one with" his world. Man in a sense
was indistinguishable from and dependent upon his world.
The whole of his existence was couched in a sacred framework of forces and events over which he had no control. However, there was always the danger that man would resort to
magic to explain and control other people and his world. In
the ontological stage the attempt was made to isolate sub-
stances, subject from object. The central issue was to discover
what something was — to probe its relationship to the source
of reality.

Van Peursen feels that man has now arrived at the functional period of history. Man no longer discovers nature to
be the realm of mysterious and overwhelming powers. The
challenge is no longer that of probing the deeper questions
of the origin and meaning of life. Rather, man's concern is
with the function which nature plays in his life — how it can
be shaped and used to make his life better. Reality becomes
that which plays a particular temporary function.[4]

Harvey Cox took the schema provided by the Comte and
Van Peursen pattern and reformulated it into sociological
jargon. Cox considers the same trend from the theological
or mythical to the pragmatic to have defined man's habitat
as well; namely, the flow from tribal village to the town, and

eventually to the modern metropolis — The Secular City. Accordingly, because the metaphysical age has passed, man is left to his own pragmatic resources to make it in the marketplace.

The attempt on the part of Cox to show the relationship between man's thought structures and the environment which he constructs and in which he lives is extremely suggestive. The bold affirmation of the city as the place where the challenges and possibilities of the future are the greatest stands in stark contrast to the underlying suspicion and basic uneasiness which members of the "Sacred Against the Secular" stance held toward the city.

The faith-filled pragmatism which was found especially evident in President Kennedy is the same kind of pragmatism which Cox claims is the dominant style of the Secular City. "*Pragmatism* . . . secular man's concern with the question 'Will it work?' . . . *Profanity* . . . secular man's wholly terrestrial horizon." [5] This sense of living with the deconsecrated nature of life is described more fully in the following remark:

> Urban-secular man came to town after the funeral for the religious world-view was already over. He feels no sense of deprivation and has no interest in mourning. . . . In the age of the secular city, the questions with which we concern ourselves tend to be mostly functional and operational.[6]

Although the model which Cox holds forth is most suggestive, one is haunted by the thought that "it ain't necessarily so!" That is, one wonders whether it is possible to find a significant number of such secular men walking the streets of Chicago, or any city for that matter. Beyond that, is it possible to make the claim that secular men have not lived in previous stages of history such as tribal Israel? Is it not possible that there could have been a secular tribe or a secular town? The thought of Cox and Comte is dependent upon a philosophy which shows history intently grinding out its aim from mythical to pragmatic. Is history that irreversible? Is it not possible to return occasionally to a more "sacred" orientation or mentality?

In reviewing a study conducted in 1965 for the *Catholic Digest*, Martin Marty points out that the secular man of Harvey Cox is difficult to find. Whoever listens to "the man on the street," watches celebrities on late-night television, or reads widely will not always encounter the cool, sunny, happy, pragmatic-empirical agnostic — the secular man. Rather, the man whom the Gallup Poll discovered believes in a God, whether Father or force, who certainly is a God who serves the purposes of man.[7]

The "Gallup man" expects everybody to believe deeply in his religion yet does not think less of nonbelievers. He encourages people to attend the church of their choice and yet considers his church to have a guiding influence in his life. The Gallup man, in fact, can become most religious especially when the going gets rough. He is, however, as interested in comfort as in his eternal destiny and wants churches to be more concerned with teaching a good way of life than with working for spiritual conversion. Although Gallup's Protestant man considers religion to be slightly less important than it was fifteen years ago, he is deeply troubled by people lacking the sense of right and wrong which they used to have.[8]

What Marty sees in the findings of this poll is reinforced by a sound understanding of American history. Pietistic religion is deeply ingrained in the American cultural ethos and more than a little secularization is needed to root it out. Just as Comte failed to bring in the positivistic kingdom, so, too, more than talking about modern man "come of age" will be needed to produce secular man in any sizable numbers. What may be occurring in the American scene is a shifting of religious loyalties rather than their disappearance. That religion is not formally identified with every aspect of human life is true, but not new. That man in his public and private life does not live up to the ideals of his religious beliefs is true, but may not be sufficient grounds for a new theology. The extent to which religious faith and religious organizations influence the lives of men in the developing urban scene is difficult to discern.

In spite of such criticisms of *The Secular City* as those which have been mentioned, Cox has laid a legitimate challenge on our theological doorstep. The need for an urban theology which grows out of the ever-present reality and complexity of the city cannot be minimized. A theology which addresses the situation of the man who is caught up in the pragmatic squeeze play of the capitalistic system is needed. A theology which leaves behind the "sweet Jesus" of agrarian pastoral bliss and forges ahead into the rugged, competitive terrain of urban life in behalf of the "bitter Christ" is demanded!

Who is secular man? With *The Secular City* echoing in our ears we can claim that he is the man who risks being shaped and determined by the cultural expressions and patterns of life which the total society has helped to create. This risk means an openness to the urban-technological setting which invades every part of our lives and is the warp and woof of our fabric of existence. Carl Jung has well described this modern man-come-of-age:

> I must say that the man we call modern, the man who is aware of the immediate present, is by no means the average man. He is rather the man who stands upon a peak, or at the very edge of the world, the abyss of the future before him, above him the heavens, and below him the whole of mankind with a history that disappears in primeval mists. The modern man — or, let us say again, the man of the immediate present — is rarely met with. There are few who live up to the name, for they must be conscious to a superlative degree. Since to be wholly of the present means to be fully conscious of one's existence as a man, it requires the most intensive and extensive consciousness, with a minimum of unconsciousness. It must be clearly understood that the mere fact of living in the present does not make a man modern, for in that case everyone at present alive would be so. He alone is modern who is fully conscious of the present.[9]

THE PROCESS OF SECULARIZATION

"Secularization is an ambiguous word which describes an ambivalent process."   C. F. Von Weizäcker[10]

The historical pegs upon which one might hang the sources of and impetus for this process of secularization include the scope of recorded history. Whether one even believes that there is such an "animal" as the process of secularization depends upon how the description is being done, by whom, for whom, and in what context. Even the rationalizing of ancient myths by the Greek philosophers can be interpreted as a step in the process of secularization. Certainly, the construction of a rational structure of the cosmos by Aristotle helped to lay the groundwork for an objective consideration of the world. By distinguishing between faith and reason,

Thomas of Aquinas carried the work of Aristotle forward to the threshold of the modern age. The Renaissance, Reformation, and all of the political, social, scientific, and technological revolutions which have followed have contributed to the atmosphere in which man feels free to manipulate his world.

In contrast to the stance taken by Ellul toward the process of secularization one finds a man like Van Leeuwen embracing the technological process as if it were the incarnation of the Christian tradition. Indeed, he considers the forces at work in the process of secularization to be the twentieth-century manifestation of missionary impetus in the Christian tradition.

In *Christianity in World History* Van Leeuwen interprets the peculiarly dynamic character of Western civilization and its worldwide effect, particularly in the present revolutionary stage of technology, as a crisis for all religion. Because Western civilization was formed and driven forward by the dynamic spirit of Christianity, it is better equipped to deal with and accept the process of secularization than is the Eastern world with its stress on the inward life and intuitive thinking.

In order to build his case Van Leeuwen attempts to ground his interpretation of the causes of the process of secularization in the biblical understanding of the Judaeo-Christian tradition. First of all, Van Leeuwen stresses that in the creation account history is discovered. Where there is a covenant established between Creator and creation, between the Lord and his people, the solid oneness of the universe is burst open. Gone is the understanding of man who is at one with his world. "Here there is proper room for man and here the taste of freedom. The world is now radically secularized" and becomes "the arena of history." [11]

Van Leeuwen maintains that the Old Testament bears witness to the basic shift which occurred in the story by which the Hebrews found meaning in their experience. They gradually shifted away from a view of the world as a cosmic totality. A world in which the divine power was one step removed from the immediacy of magic and taboo was left behind for the God who was one and transcendent. This change in understanding is clearly seen in the understanding of the role of the king in Israel. While neighboring countries such as Egypt continued to claim that the king was divine, Israel's men of faith only reluctantly gave her a king and continued to hold him under prophetic judgment. Cox refers to this as the *"desacralization of politics."* [12]

Taking the same biblical themes Von Weizsäcker further develops the manner in which the Judaeo-Christian tradition prepared the way for contemporary scientific research. Von Weizsäcker sees the sense of freedom from the gods as a primary ingredient in man's willingness to subdue nature. In the biblical tradition, "God now is so highly exalted above the whole world, everything in the world is of the same nature: it is a creature of God, it is not God. Thus God himself has deprived the world of its divinity." [13]

Von Weizsäcker sees in the Genesis accounts of creation the terrifying demand of faith in one God which frees the Hebrew from the relativities and the monstrosities of polytheism. This faith took man out of a world of "manyness" and plurality. It set him squarely in the midst of a sensible and rational historical process in which he was given responsibility for the created order. Add to this the New Testament understanding of the Incarnation which revealed a God who considered the stuff of the world worthy of his love, and the man of faith is provided with a sufficient grounding for becoming a responsible agent in God's creative process. [14]

Although we may not be convinced that the Judaeo-Christian tradition was mainly responsible for the secularizing forces which contributed to scientific inquiry, we must agree that there is within the tradition the ingredients necessary for such thought and technological development.

Van Leeuwen and Von Weizsäcker spelled out the manner in which the Judaeo-Christian tradition could have been the major contributor toward scientific-technological development in the Western world, but Friedrich Gogarten has developed the most comprehensive understanding of the man of faith in this process. Gogarten's central thesis is that the historical process of secularization is the logical and appropriate outcome of the responsibility for the world bestowed on man by the Christian faith. Thus, according to Gogarten, if those tutored in the Christian tradition were not primarily responsible for secularization, they should have been!

Gogarten has endeavored to think through the problem of theology and history exclusively within the context of secularization. For Gogarten secularization is far more than a mere catchword; it is a sign of hope and crisis which demands a radical reformation of the entire theological enterprise.[15]

The essential element of secularization, according to Gogarten, is the transformation of institutions, ideas, and experiences that were once the work of divine providence into the product of purely human thought and action. Like Van Leeuwen and Von Weizsäcker he considers this transformed relation to the world to have occurred in the prophetic preaching of Judaism and Christianity. Man needed to be freed from the understanding that he was enslaved by cosmic forces in order that he might accept responsibility for mentally ordering his world and physically subduing the natural resources of the world.[16]

This transformed relation is experienced at two levels according to Gogarten. Man has been freed from the sense of being tied to his world in some kind of mythical unity so that he might take on responsibility for that world. As a man of faith he has also witnessed a change in his Christian ideas and experiences. He is no longer primarily oriented to a divine ground. As a secularized Christian he accepts much of his previous experience as a Christian in more human categories of understanding.[17] Larry Shiner, who has done extensive study on the thought of Gogarten, calls this process "a secularization of Christian secularity."

The fundamental distinction which must be made concerning the contributions of Gogarten is the difference between making historical claims for causality and providing a theological understanding of the process of secularization. It is doubtful whether one can maintain a historical causality between the Judaeo-Christian tradition and the development of the process of secularization in the Western culture. A good case can be made, contrary to Gogarten, that the recovery of the great thinkers of antiquity during the Renaissance and Enlightenment periods of history was the element which stimulated the development of the process of secularization in modern times.[18]

Although it is hard to accept as *historically* accurate Gogarten's contention that Christian faith stands in a causal relationship to secularization, his *theological* argument that faith is not only compatible with secularization but demands its continuance, remains intact.[19]

Nevertheless, there are reasons why particular expressions of a culture become dominant and are passed along from one generation to the next. The mental outlook and faith stance of a people affect what they are capable of pursuing and accepting. Changes in a culture are integrally related to the capacities of a people to understand and encompass such changes. This close relationship or affinity which exists between the theological ideas or mental framework and the scientific or technological achievements, for example, of a given society or culture must be studied carefully. The dynamic and fluid relationship between what might be called the world of symbols and ideas and the world of concrete cultural expression is crucial for an understanding of what is happening in our world. Shiner calls this continual transformation of a culture "intellectual-existential." It is intellectual in that new ideas or values arrive on the scene along with accompanying changes in the material and physical realm. And it is existential in that a new environment within which one lives out one's existence addresses and shapes one's entire person.[20]

Gogarten's conception of secularization as the transformation of institutions, ideas, and experiences that were once the work of divine providence into the product of purely human thought and action may be misleading. There is confusion as to where the mutation takes place. Is it in divine providence as such? Is it in the function which the Christian understanding of the world has had? Is it a change in man's existential stance toward the world? Gogarten seems to claim that shifts, which demand a secular stance on the part of the man of faith, have occurred because of divine providence (the Incarnation, for example).

Jarrett-Kerr levels a criticism in terms of historical causality when he asks the question of Gogarten, "What if the derivation of secularization from the Christian doctrine of God and creation is itself challenged?" Jarrett-Kerr is particularly concerned about what he sees in Gogarten's thought as the elevation of secularization as a child of Christianity from a tentative historical judgment into a theological absolute.[21]

It is one thing to affirm with Gogarten that the Judaeo-Christian tradition has been responsible for the injection into history of new possibilities for existence such as a positive estimate of nature and man's responsibility for the created order. But it is quite another thing to claim that the Christian tradition can claim sole parentage of the process of secularization. History is too complex a phenomenon for anyone to make such a claim.

In relating this discussion to the "Sacred-Secular Paradox" stance as such, we are reminded of a Barthian fallacy — the tendency to perceive the theological "ideal" to be *one* with the historical or cultural "fact." To point up the similarity between aspects of the Judaeo-Christian tradition and some expressions in history is quite different from positing a causal relationship between them. This tendency may be rooted, for example, in Barth's understanding of the all-pervasive nature of the Christ in our world. But what may be said to be a theological position must be cautiously distinguished from what is really the case in real historical life.

The credit for popularizing the thinking and contributions of Gogarten must go to Cox's *The Secular City*. Cox brought secularization into the American home through this very readable book. Cox translated Gogarten's theological categories into sociological ones as he saw the transformed relation of man to his world to be taking place most definitely in the city.

> Secularization . . . marks a change in the way men grasp and understand their life together, and it occurred only when the cosmopolitan confrontations of city living exposed the relativity of the myths and traditions men once thought were unquestionable. . . . The secular metropolis stands as . . . a field of human exploration and endeavor from which the gods have fled.[22]

The city is the place where man has been liberated from religious and metaphysical tutelage — in Bonhoeffer's terminology, "come of age." The urban, secular man, according to Cox, has turned his attention away from the world beyond and has set his sights upon this world and this time.

The contributions of Cox and Gogarten have not gone without rebuttal. The reactions have usually followed a predictable pattern of criticizing Cox and Gogarten either for their understanding of history or for their use of the biblical faith. Both of these men have been accused of pulling the cloak of theological respectability about the process of secularization through reference to particular passages of Scripture and misuse of certain traditional doctrines. George Peck, for example, questions whether it is possible to bring the world of the biblical writers into the modern secular society without overlooking some fundamental differences. The direct marriage of certain biblical themes and the findings of sociological and historical studies cannot be that conveniently performed. In fact, it may be accomplished under circumstances usually associated with "shotgun weddings"! Although these efforts to unite the Bible and history are conducted in an attempt to overcome what Reinhold Niebuhr once called the "transcendental irresponsibility" of neoorthodoxy, one must question their exaggerated rush to embrace the secular outlook as having foundations in the Bible itself.

In terms of the correctness with which the process of secularization is said to have already taken place, we refer again to the comments of Martin Marty that the religious atmosphere in America just does not bear out what is being said in such treatises as *The Secular City*. If the process of secularization is as relentless as men such as Gogarten, Van Leeuwen, and Cox maintain, then there is a serious case of "retardation" or "cultural lag" on the American scene in this regard. Marty maintains that an understanding of secularization which maintains a mono-dimensional, mono-directional picture is on shaky ground at best. Within the United States the possibilities of religious change are much more pluralistic and open.[23] The religious changes during the last twenty years have not been large. But given the understanding of the depth of the predetermining matrix of American life (Evangelical-Conservative Civic Religion) which holds on to the status quo like a bulldog, the slight shift in religious attitudes may reflect the beginning of a more fundamental reorientation than is presently observable.

We may well be on the verge of post-Christianity! Technology, the communications media, the racial revolution, and increased affluence are forcing a new perception on contemporary man. But significant changes have not yet been observed in the patterns of expressed belief and behavior of the American religious individual.

Whether the contemporary world is secular is still undecided. Whether the Judaeo-Christian tradition has been primarily responsible for the present condition of Western culture is an even more delicate mystery. Nevertheless, the persons who represent the "Sacred-Secular Paradox" position have placed this secular agenda before us. They have provided us with the possibilities of not only affirming our world but of so doing as men of faith living in a rather sound biblical-theological framework.

The "Sacred-Secular Paradox" has called us to accept and celebrate the secular. The Christian faith from this perspective not only is compatible with secularization but positively demands its continuance and expansion into all areas of life in order that faith can remain genuine. The man of faith must be willing to live with the ambiguities of history. To choose to interpret the contemporary scene through the use of religious categories derived from another century (the "Sacred Against the Secular," for example) is no option. A refusal to enter the intellectual marketplace is a rejection of the mandate given to us by the Christian faith.

We must move beyond the contributions of neoorthodoxy, however. If we are to really take our world seriously, we must deal with a basic Barthian problem — the split between faith and reason.

> Neo-orthodoxy, having founded itself on a belief in a sharp separation between the wisdom of man and the wisdom of God, had no alternative except to be unclear as to the meaning of its message and program, or to become so orthodox (that is, so reflective of the theology of Protestant scholasticism and the theology of the nineteenth-century American Church) as to become irrelevant to the modern situation. It thus became as harmless as the dove without the wisdom of the serpent.[24]

Obviously the "pop-Barth" in Harvey Cox is much too offensive for most religious aspirants in the American scene. This should not prevent us from hearing what Cox has to say. It falls upon those theologians of the next decade to build upon such efforts and move beyond the Barthian impasse if at all possible.

RELIGION AND CHRISTIANITY

Barth's suspicion of religion is still bothering contemporary Barthians. Bonhoeffer and Gogarten illustrate this position by drawing a sharp distinction between all religion and the Christian faith. A theme which is common to both of these men has been the schism in the theological understanding of the law-gospel motif. Bonhoeffer claimed that there is both a divine and a human history in the Christ event. This distinction betrays a definite concern to maintain the distinction between God and the world so that God may be God and the world may retain its "worldly" character.

If the contributions of these men are not to dissipate into just another expression of avant-gardism, then there is theological work to be done. Their contribution to the discussion of "religionless Christianity" has become the battle cry of many a well-meaning theological interpreter of the contemporary secular confusion. Current efforts to prevent the church from becoming too "churchy" or religious are grounded in Barth's and Bonhoeffer's efforts to "de-religionize" Christianity.

Disciples of Bonhoeffer have uttered many strange pronouncements based upon the above understanding. The following comments are examples of the attempts to echo the theme of religionless Christianity and set forth a worldly faith:

> The coming of Jesus Christ in this modern world will be a secular event or it will not happen at all.[25]

> It is here that we must ask what the Christian faith means by its claim that in a secular event — the life of Jesus of Nazareth — the meaning of history has come into the midst of history.[26]

> The Coming of Christ is a secular event. It is an event in the world and for the world. And consequently this secular event and what was invited by it, the thing we usually call Christianity, cannot be anything else but a secular movement, a movement in the world and for the world.[27]

Behind such "secularizing" rhetoric, one may discover an honest attempt to purify the Christian tradition according to the principles set forth by Bonhoeffer or Barth.

In order to gain a clearer understanding of this attempt to find a pure Christianity, let us look a bit more closely at what Bonhoeffer conceived religion to be. In his *Letters and Papers from Prison* we gain a vivid understanding of the contempt in which he held the contemporary religious piety of fellow Germans.

> Our whole nineteen-hundred-year-old Christian preaching and theology rests upon the "religious premise" of man. . . . What is the significance of a Church . . . in a religionless world? . . . How do we speak . . . in a secular fashion of God? . . . I often ask myself why a Christian instinct frequently draws me more to the religionless than to the religious. . . .[28]

These remarks are grounded in Bonhoeffer's suspicion of a religious inwardness and an individualized, privatized religious practice which was common in the German church.

But there seems to be more at stake than merely this desire to cleanse the faith of outdated forms of piety. Involved in Bonhoeffer's understanding of religion is his claim that man's religious sensitivities have undergone a great change. Gone are the metaphysical-religious *a priori*'s which enabled the Christian to have the inside track to God! The world's "coming of age" has left the church as a useless appendage in society as long as it still operates as a religious organization.

Does Bonhoeffer mean that modern man can no longer comprehend traditional forms of Christian theology because of a structural change in his mental capacities, or does he mean that a change of terminology is needed to make the old traditions more palatable? Bonhoeffer was supporting a redefinition of traditional theology and church life to make them more relevant to what he considered to be the needs of humanity. Because he saw the activity of the church too often concerned with the periphery of man's existence and increasingly crowded from the center of activity, he challenged the institutional church to de-religionize, and he called upon theology to become secular enough to be able to relate to the needs of man. These demands upon the church were not merely academic! Bonhoeffer saw the future of the church threatened unless it woke up to the challenges of the world's coming of age.

Bonhoeffer called churchmen to free themselves of their obsessions with outward expressions of religiosity and begin to live life as it was. By just being open to life a Christian would develop a sensitivity toward the needs of people and an awareness of the mission of the church. Bonhoeffer must have seen the church and contemporary Christians as the proverbial "see no evil, hear no evil" monkey. With their fingers in their ears and their hands over their eyes, the church of Germany of the 1930's was marching naïvely into history.

Bonhoeffer vigorously attacked the religious individualism which attempted to keep the Christian faith "boxed-in" and the world and its turmoil "boxed-out." The man of faith who kept his understanding of the faith in an unthreatened compartment of his life rather than exposing it at the center of his existence was most despicable to this martyr of the German church who knew what it would cost to really "keep the faith." A God of the gaps at the edges of life was as repulsive to Bonhoeffer as that faith stance was to Hebrew prophet Amos who spoke of a God who found little delight in the religious celebrations of the unrighteous and the unjust.

Bonhoeffer's criticism of religion must be seen within the context of the German church and the German world of the 1930's. Because he saw the German church against the drama of world history, which was being ground out to the beat of the German armies, his somewhat cynical response to the church is more easily understood. However, his martyr spirit has enabled his witness to transcend national boundaries so that we too must hear about the dangers of religious acculturation. As we discovered in the previous discussion concerning the "Sacred Against the Secular" type and its influence upon American civic religious life, we need to hear Bonhoeffer's warnings.

The contemporary prophet in the Amos tradition who has stood up in the marketplace and in fact has come crashing into the sanctuary (heaven forbid!) is James Forman. The Black Manifesto which he laid before the church in America has the same roots as the probing quest of Bonhoeffer: the church needs to de-religionize. That is, it needs to be made aware of both the demands of its faith and its complicity with evil structures in the contemporary society. The Manifesto just reemphasizes that the task of Bonhoeffer needs to be undertaken again, and again, and again!

Harvey Cox took over Bonhoeffer's definition of religion as dependency, inwardness, and reliance upon a supernaturalism which sees this world somehow subsumed within another one. This concept lies behind such statements as, "The technological metropolis provides the indispensable social setting for a world of 'no religion at all.'"[29] Cox may have redefined religion and relocated its center of operation, but a religious concern still exists in the way he uses biblical themes to interpret the secular phenomenon. In interpreting secularization as the logical result of the influence of biblical categories and God as the one who supplies the framework or limitation within which freedom alone has any meaning, Cox has reinstated the religious dimension. To affirm that secular man *can* experience the transcendent and order his world around it is to reintroduce the category of religion. Therefore, because modern man still asks those questions formerly called ultimate questions, we are forced to conclude that *homo religiosus* is not dead.[30]

Because Cox may not have been convincing enough to rid the man of faith of those forms of religiosity which are coercive, individualistic, and idolatrous, this task unfinished or otherwise is laid on us. Whether we live in a city which is secular or pagan, whether we live in a world which is maturing, "come of age," or regressing, we are obliged as men of faith to wrestle with the issues of religionless Christianity which are a part of any church institution which exists in this world.

Thus the echoes of "religionless Christianity" are still heard in our midst. Karl Barth has indelibly stamped the polarization of religion and Christian faith upon contemporary religious culture. The faith which is pure stands in judgment upon every form of religion including Christianity. Barth's distinction between religion and faith was not so much based upon descriptive observation of contemporary religious life as it was upon decisively theological grounds. Barth's fundamental concern was that whether men are more or less religious, or even totally lack a sense of the sacred, they are neither nearer to nor farther from the revelation of God in Jesus Christ. This is the "paradox" of faith as Barth saw it. The same paradox is ingrained in the position which we have designated as the "Sacred-Secular Paradox."

This Barthian paradox still hangs like an ominous cloud hovering over the contemporary church scene. Barth's attack on all forms of religious constructs remains with us. But we must ask him and his followers: "Is it possible to keep the faith apart from religious embodiment? Is it possible to speak of God apart from the utilization of concrete historical events and cultural forms?"

CONCLUDING REMARKS

We have paid our visit to the "secular city." We have taken a long look at the best of dreams of the old men and the finest of theological visions of the young. Even now the halos from the secular saints are becoming tarnished. Their visions have been challenged and probed by the best of men and by the worst of men. In the words of Martin Marty:

> The Secular City did turn out to be Camelot; the new creation which was metropolis turned out to be an ungovernable and is now a burning entity. Secular man is no longer in control; for a time he was even seen trailing off behind yogis and gurus.[31]

Nevertheless, the best which is in us and the more hope-filled of our moments cling to the vision which is like a hoped-for victory which has been taken from us by a field goal in the last seconds. We stand at the empty tomb, for we too celebrated the death of the forms of the church which Bonhoeffer and Cox have celebrated. We stand before the stone which was rolled away looking for and longing to see the new thing which is come to pass! Somehow the recognition of the "resurrection event" eludes us.

The movement of theological thought has carried the contributions of men from the "Sacred-Secular Paradox" far downstream. Their contributions to the ongoing process are not minimized. But the theological solutions to the church's problems have once more slipped out of our grasp. This is the nemesis of change — even the celebrators of change are frequently left homeless. The breakup of neoorthodox theologies has not yet been followed by a new, commonly accepted formulation, though there have been some creative gropings in the midst of the current theological chaos.

4
The Eclipse of the Secular

During the early 1950's, when wrestling was king, the "tag-team" match was regular Saturday evening television fare. This particular event pitted a team of two wrestlers against another team of two men. In the match, one team member could come to the aid of his partner in case he became exhausted or otherwise immobilized in the process of the match. However, the spectator could see that the two team members did not hold particular admiration for each other. They were comrades of necessity.

As we take up the theologians depicted in this chapter, we may find that they are more nearly members of one team with the individuals of the "Sacred-Secular Paradox" than we might first suspect. Although members of these two camps have spent considerable time sparring with each other over seemingly insurmountable issues, they have more in common than any two of the other styles depicted in the book. The "Sacred-Secular Paradox" half of the team tends to be suspicious of philosophical speculation as a theological enterprise. They are inclined toward accenting the "Word" in the Barthian tradition. On the other hand, the "Eclipse of the

Secular" team member attempts to justify the faith in the philosophical arena. He attempts to build as solid a bridge as possible to the secular man through use of secular disciplines. The prime example of this stance and methodology is Paul Tillich's method of correlation in which one begins to theologize at the level of understanding or current condition of one's hearers.

Although this basic disagreement has brought on some vigorous dialogue, it must not be forgotten that members of these two camps are wrestling with the same opponent — a world which has increasingly said no to the gospel.

Besides Tillich there are Mircea Eliade, Bernard Meland, and a number of lesser lights who can be considered to be participants in the "Eclipse of the Secular" or "Total Sacrality" rubric. What do we mean by "Total Sacrality"? As the title of the chapter indicates, in the thought of these men one discovers the "eclipse of the secular" taking place. Members of this group maintain that the totality of existence participates in the sacred order of things. The secular does not exist as such. It takes on meaning only as it is related to and in fact submerged in the reality of the sacred.

THE SECULAR

Probably no fear is voiced more strongly by Tillich, Eliade, and Meland than the fear that the nature of experience is somehow being stripped of its "sacral" qualities, that it is taking on the tastelessness of "everydayishness." Although man has the distinct option of doing so, these men believe that it is utterly disastrous to relate to the world in a merely profane or secular manner.

In his book *The Sacred and the Profane*, Mircea Eliade very carefully points out that there are two kinds of relationships which man can have toward his world. "*Sacred* and *profane* are two modes of being in the world, two existential situations assumed by man in the course of his history." [1] He holds that the secular has no meaning apart from the sacred. It can become the vehicle of sacral realities but it cannot sustain life on its own. Thus the secular is defined in terms of and is meaningless apart from its relation to the manifestation of the sacred in its midst. The secular "shell" is a lifeless blob apart from the vitality of the sacred. "The profane is chaos because it is the undifferentiated and therefore the unreal; but it is experienced *as* profane only so long as the sacred manifests itself." [2]

Similarly, Paul Tillich, in reference to the use of the word "secular" and the "reality" to which it refers, regards "secular" as a religious word which could only arise in a religious setting. The secular refers to the withdrawal of spheres of man from religious influence and control. "Secular" is the religious man's word to explain a situation in which the sacred is inhibited. For Tillich the word "secular" arises in the religious community in an attempt at self-understanding. For such a religious community the secular realm depicts the receding of the centers of human effort, interest, and inquiry from Christian sanction, control, and principles of interpretation.

In his further attempt to plumb the depth of the meaning of the secular, Tillich concludes that the word "secular" is less expressive than the word "profane":

> . . . which means "in front of the doors" — of the holy. . . . Everything secular is implicitly related to the holy. It can become the bearer of the holy. The divine can become manifest in it. Nothing is essentially and inescapably secular. . . . Everything secular is potentially sacred, open to consecration. [3]

For Tillich this means that secular things, events, and realms have the potential of becoming matters of ultimate concern — worthy of religious adherence. On the other hand, there is always the possibility that divine or sacred powers can be reduced to secular objects and consequently lose their religious character.

Tillich's negative evaluation of aspects of culture which have left the sacred fold is well-founded in history. He wrote against the background of a world which had just passed through the agonies of its second world war. Tillich witnessed at firsthand the destructiveness of man. He knew that people died and the righteous suffered at the hands of man. Babies were neglected and killed. Hatred seemed to conquer love. Nevertheless, he longed for the day when as a man of faith he could say that the demonic had been conquered and that the distinction between the sacred and the secular was transcended. Man experiences this ecstatic moment only occasionally, however. Such a realization of the unity of sacred and secular is, nevertheless, the aim of creation.

Coming upon the theological scene from a more American perspective, Bernard Meland holds up the shifting world situation in a slightly different light. Although the "secular" is emerging and becomes more visible than was previously the case, Meland sees this as a "revolt" which goes much deeper than just a reaction against a religious tradition or establishment. Discussing what he calls the process of "de-absolutization," Meland says the following: "Basically, it turns out to be a rejection of all historically formulated absolutes, whether religious, philosophical, or political in nature." [4]

The absolutes of which Meland speaks are not just Christian symbols. The "museum pieces" of all religions, and in fact all institutions, are being roughly treated in our day. The treasures of history are being called upon to justify themselves, or, even worse, they are ignored. We shall discover that Meland is obviously nervous about the erosion of man's "religious sensibilities" in the midst of the contemporary culture's liberating madness.

What is the secular for Meland and the others? The secular is the "spin-off" from the creative world process. But instead of reflecting and embodying the sacred, it attempts to become autonomous. The proper role of the secular is to be the vehicle of the sacred and never to take over the driver's seat. To adopt another image, the secular moon is to remain in the shadows of the sacred sun's rays. If and when its orbit comes between the sun and the world situation, it threatens the life of man. The feeling of Meland, Eliade, and Tillich is that the secular moon has, indeed, partially eclipsed the sacred sun. A total eclipse would be a fate worse than death. All that would be left would be lifeless, cold moon rocks! The maintenance of the sacred, and in fact its prominent survival, is essential to the continuation of man in a creative life situation.

The basic question which must be addressed to the adherents of the "Eclipse of the Secular" is the future market for primordial religious myth in an age which is becoming increasingly nonmythological and spiritually unidimensional; an age which sees life and reality as all on the single level of the finite.

SECULARITY

Just as the secular is considered somewhat of an illegitimate child by the adherents of the "Eclipse of the Secular," so the mind-set which dominates the secular realm is no more desirable to them. Any attempt to maintain thought forms apart from their sacred grounding is described as demonic, because it is the denial of the historical and transitory nature of institutions and cultural expressions. This ascription of a changeless, nonhistorical status to the changing world is called secularism.

Secularism is really a religious form with numerous disguises. It is a profane expression of the sacred which attempts to hide its claim of absolute authority. Another definition of secularism is to call it the attempt on the part of particular aspects of culture or persons to establish as absolute a relative idea or mentality.

Tillich's understanding of the divorce of life from its sacred ground is related to the context of what he saw happening in the industrialization of society. In much the same manner as Ellul feared the re-creation of man into the image of the machine, Tillich warned of the transformation of everything, including man himself, into an object of calculation and control. Tillich thus interpreted secularism in terms of existential alienation. Tillich spoke of this "emptiness" in the following manner: ". . . the emptiness of adjustment to the demands of the industrial society, and the emptiness of cultural goods without ultimate seriousness, lead to indifference, cynicism, despair, mental disturbances, early crimes, disgust of life." [5]

The demonic nature of contemporary industrial society is seen in those places where man has become a part of the reality he has created, an object among objects, to which he must adapt himself in order not to be destroyed. Out of this predicament of man in the industrial society the experiences of emptiness and meaninglessness, of dehumanization and estrangement have resulted. Such a man has ceased to encounter life as meaningful.

Tillich wanted the dynamic and mystery of life to be expressed. His understanding of secularism is that it shuts man off from the depths of life. If a "total eclipse" of the depths of life takes place, man may well find himself alienated from the processes of culture, the meaning of himself, and alienated from the basis of life itself — God.

Tillich's stance toward the secular mentality is a legitimate warning against allowing the industrial and technological order or man's capitalistic interests to define the shape of society. In a day when men at all levels of society are joyously celebrating the gifts of freedom and the expansion of knowledge, we must affirm the need to keep in mind the relativity of everything. Those who are plumbing the depths and complexities of life are learning a new humility as they discover the limited nature of their understanding.

If contemporary man can transcend the biases and vested interests of the past, if he can refuse to establish any absolutes, then his life experience might well avoid the demonic nature of a closed, absolutizing, and futureless secularism.

THE PROCESS OF SECULARIZATION

If one maintains that the basis of reality is to be found in the sacred, then the process of secularization as essentially a process of the eclipse of the sacred will not be welcomed. This process of "desacralization" has neutralized nature and human life and left modern man living almost totally in the profane, that is, in mere history.

Mircea Eliade is particularly dismayed at the desacralization which pervades the entire experience of the nonreligious man of modern societies. Such an individual finds it increasingly difficult to rediscover the deeply experiential dimensions of religious man, of *homo religiosus*. If the theological enterprise were to accept Eliade's understanding of secularization, it would embark on a course designed to promote a rebirth of the sacred mode of existence. To develop Eliade's line of thought further would mean to admit that the Christian faith is fundamentally involved in the sacred realm of existence. Eliade calls for the revival of the "cosmic dimension" in Christianity in which one might experience a deep existential participation in the cosmos.[6]

However, Eliade does not seem to have understood correctly the biblical tradition. In biblical history man is grounded in the dynamic, ongoing process of history. To live out of that kind of faith story means that one must live with diversity and plurality. One is not primarily accountable for maintaining a sacred orientation toward life.

The most sophisticated effort to set forth a positive estimate of secularization from the perspective which we have designated as the "Eclipse of the Secular" is to be found in the theology of Paul Tillich. Tillich's position is that the religious-secular dialectic is grounded in an ultimate unity. Radical secularism can abolish particular functions or expressions of religion but it cannot destroy religion as a quality of "ultimate concern." However, Tillich considers secular autonomy to have triumphed sufficiently for him to speak of a "sacred void" in contemporary life. Yet for Tillich, as is the case for Eliade, there can be no truly nonreligious man, since there is "no place *beside* the divine, there is no possible atheism, there is no wall between the religious and the nonreligious. The holy embraces both itself and the secular." [7] This statement is a very clear definition of what we mean by the "Eclipse of the Secular" in the thought of Tillich.

The struggle which is going on in human history is cast by Tillich in the highly technical schema of autonomy-heteronomy-theonomy. The autonomous person or thrust in history responds to rational criteria which one finds in oneself as a rational being. This drive toward independence is opposed by the heteronomous forces — external demands as to how reason should grasp and shape reality. "The basis of a genuine heteronomy is the claim to speak in the name of the ground of being and therefore in an unconditional and ultimate way." [8] If man is genuinely sensitive and open to that in which his life is ultimately grounded, then his most profound concerns can be said to be rooted in the Being of God.

Both autonomy, man's response to reason, and heteronomy, the demands placed upon man by his environment, are rooted in theonomy — the depth of reason. To discover and participate in this dimension of life is to discover the nature of *agape* and the expression of God's love in the Christian community. To be "world-affirming" without being concerned to ground one's life in the Depths of Life (the Ground of Being or God) is to flirt with life at a superficial level. Tillich's criticism of many of the attempts to affirm that the process of secularization is grounded in the Judaeo-Christian tradition would be that this same process is prone to dissolve the holy into the secular — to pave the way for a total seculari- zation of Christian culture.[9]

With Tillich the process of secularization is not a monolithic reality steadily grinding away at expressions of theonomy (manifestations of God) in culture. The process of seculari- zation can rather be found at varying degrees of intensity and stages of development depending upon what particular facet of culture one is observing.

Although Bernard Meland has a more "secular" tone in his language, he is very close to Tillich in his understanding of the process of secularization and what it means for the man of faith. Instead of speaking of the erosion of the "theonomous" nature of human existence, he refers to the "movement away from traditionally accepted norms and sensibilities." [10]

Meland considers the process of secularization to be tran- spiring at different rates and to have developed to different degrees depending upon the culture under observation. Mel- and's more flexible portrayal of the process of secularization is indeed helpful. He considers the reaction against the in- herited religious beliefs in the early phase of the modern period in the Western world to have been unique. In other parts of the contemporary world secularization is identified with those social forces which are attempting to liberate and cleanse particular societies of totalitarian or dictatorial forms of government. Meland sees the process of secularization within contemporary cultures taking place under a variety of conditions and against backgrounds of cultural traditions that range from the primitive to the highly developed forms of civilization.[11]

The basic threat which Meland sees in the process of secu- larization is in the maintenance of historical or religious "sensi- bilities."

> Secularization is not an overt interpretation of man, but a condition that befalls him or his culture when the spiritual challenge to his sentient and psychical life is dissipated through trivial absorptions, or when it is set aside through exposure to processes of society which cancel out all consideration of the human being as a reality worthy in himself and answerable to an ultimate destiny.[12]

The image which comes to mind is that of an artist or some

other highly sensitive person being overly exposed to the ravages and brutalities of war. In a very real sense such an event could eclipse or short-circuit the historical sensitivities of such a person. What Meland, along with Tillich and Eliade, is saying is that contemporary man is being exposed to life at too trivial a level. He thus may become numbed to the more significant and ultimate of life's issues.

The "historical sensibilities" of which Meland speaks are man's fundamental ability to develop and maintain his sensitivities toward all aspects of life. Meland is counseling us to be cautious about involving ourselves in those barbarous or historically shallow expressions which dull the senses. Man's capacity to respond to esthetic and emotional stimuli must be cherished and nurtured, according to Meland. Man's ability to preserve and internalize those value systems, structures of human perception and feeling, and styles of living which are the best in a culture must be strengthened. Meland fears that the process of secularization may sever the contemporary expressions of culture from their historic roots. This separation may endanger the continued existence of indispensable values and patterns of behavior which draw their lifeblood in a sense from their grounding in history. Although each generation goes about the task of updating and reformulating the cultural tradition handed down to it, Meland considers the contemporary disdain for historical formulations and judgments to be cause for alarm.

In spite of this grave threat to contemporary man's grounding in history, Meland considers that the current revolutionary ferment in our culture may provide the occasion for the cleansing and reclaiming of our religious sensibilities. Thus the man of faith views contemporary history as having a "Janus face." On the one side it is erupting with radical innovations in the area of human awareness and expectation due to scientific achievement and cultural revolution; on the other side, contemporary history's quest for meaning may drive man to discover insights into the nature of human existence which may enable him to recover "sensibilities" previously lost.[13]

In the process of flexing its muscles the contemporary expression of culture may break off some of the shackles of the past as well as develop and discover some new muscle and insight. In the process we may find a grounding in life which will better sustain us and broaden our imaginative ability to deal with the contemporary scientific-technological revolution. The need to develop and cherish the imaginative potentiality and "awareness quotient" of man is crucial. As the church probes the dimensions of life which support and thrive on the symbolic and the artistic, she may well find herself aiding her own cause by recovering meanings attached to her ancient symbols and traditions. As long as this task does not deteriorate into one of preserving the museum pieces of faith, the church may well continue to be the vessel which is best equipped both to embody the wisdom of history and to appreciate the contemporary expressions of culture. The thought of Meland in this regard is certainly adequate to sustain a continual critique of secularization in its many forms.

Although the process of secularization seems to defy description, one can claim that there are processes within each new expression of culture which produce the "acids of modernity" which continue to eat away at the "treasures of history." Even the most antiseptic of packaging cannot protect the museum pieces of history from exposure to the pervasive character of these "acids" in our contemporary society. The biological, social, and ethical implications of modern science and technology cannot be avoided. In an age when heart transplants have become commonplace and chemical-biological warfare threatens to undo us, the man of faith has no place to hide. The increasing number of those who are willing to take responsibility for the created order must be joined by concerned churchmen.

The observation that we are in the midst of an age when man's mentality and social setting are being radically reshaped is not unique. However, the whole process of secularization, which catches up so much of the drama which we call "life," calls men of faith to dust off their rusty swords and do battle on behalf of the Lord of history. The eclipse of familiar certainties makes this task more difficult than before but all the more necessary. The role of the responsible Christian agent and institution is that of entering the marketplace of our society with persuasive power and with sensitivity. In this struggle with the world we may be able to discover just which historical patterns of living and thinking need to be preserved and strengthened and which ones need to be eliminated.

What made sense to previous generations may now be the deserved recipient of mockery. The life-style of the church is no exception. As we find ourselves unable to cope with the complexities of our age, we must strive to reformulate a reservoir of thought and tradition which can understand and celebrate the total life of man. This grasp of life will continue to be elusive. But if we are to establish and interpret the word of God in history, then we must make clear the meaning of the celebration by our contemporary world of the presence of the Lord of history.

RELIGION AND CHRISTIANITY

In sharp contrast to the other wing of neoorthodoxy which calls for and celebrates the withering away of religion stands the thought of Meland, Tillich, and Eliade. The stance of Tillich and Eliade in particular is that the decay of religion in the modern world is the sign of a failure in the human consciousness, a failure caused by the one-sided development of culture in the West. What causes this sharp divergence in opinion between these two dominant thrusts of neoorthodoxy? The key to understanding this difference lies in their understanding of the transcendence of God. For the Barthian, God's transcendence calls for the liberation of the world from religious absolutes. To be religious is only to find alternatives to faith in the Transcendent One. On the other hand, the thought of Tillich, Meland, and Eliade is closer to process theology, which holds that God's transcendence is discovered in the depths of life and not in some other realm. Religion is thus the very substance of culture! Religious symbols and traditions are the lifeblood of any creative and vibrant society.

Eliade not only repudiates any notion of destroying religious symbolism, but he also is intent upon preserving *homo religiosus* — religious man. The religious man believes that there is an absolute reality, the sacred, which transcends this world but which, nevertheless, manifests itself in this world. The sacred is present to sanctify life as well as to make it more real. The religious man is truly at home in the world.

In contrast to the religious man, Eliade characterizes the nonreligious modern man as one who regards himself to be in charge of every life situation. This man considers himself to be the subject and agent of history and refuses all appeal to transcendence. Indeed, he:

> ... *makes himself,* and he only makes himself completely in proportion as he desacralizes himself and the world. The sacred is the prime obstacle to his freedom. He will become himself only when he is totally demysticized. He will not be truly free until he has killed the last god.[14]

Just as Eliade considers nature to have become progressively secularized, so nonreligious man has undergone an analogous change. Such a modern man has committed religious and historical suicide, according to Eliade.

In spite of his attempt to remove evidences of the sacred from the world and transcendence from his life, modern man is continually haunted by the sacred "realities" he has refused and denied. Eliade likens this tragic loss of religious sensitivity to a new "fall" of man. For Eliade, the philosopher, the psychologist, and even the theologian must reintegrate a religious vision of life which enables man to ground himself in the depths of life.[15]

Eliade maintains that man becomes aware of the sacred because it manifests itself, shows itself, as something wholly different from the secular order. There is nothing in the created order which is not capable of embodying the sacred. Thus, the religious man is called upon to establish a relationship with the transcendent realities in every conceivable place in which he lives out his life.[16] Eliade's position in this regard is in direct conflict with efforts of the Barthians or the "Sacred-Secular Paradox" adherents to strip the created order of the religious so that God might be God. Eliade would oppose any attempt to "de-religionize" because the religious ingredients in a culture are the tangible expression of the cosmic or the transcendent. The *homo religiosus* is best equipped to confront life in all its depth. To destroy the religious dimension and to bring in a secularized world would leave little room for a genuine Christian faith, since a truly secular world would not be able to sustain the religious dimension. From Eliade's perspective the modern epoch is not a world "come of age" but a temporary relapse. The sooner that we are removed from this eclipse of the sacred the better. Whether we can respond to Eliade's call for the return of a sacred mode of living seems doubtful.

The theologian who has most energetically incorporated the concept of religion into his thought is Paul Tillich. He has many similarities with Eliade but goes beyond him at a number of points. Tillich maintains that religion is not only a necessary ingredient in the spiritual life, but that the expression of religion cannot be avoided. The choice is not *whether* but *how* one is going to be religious. "You cannot reject religion with ultimate seriousness, because ultimate seriousness, or the state of being ultimately concerned, is itself religion." [17] Tillich considers the religious surge in life to be so much a part of the warp and woof of things that even the attempts to destroy the presence of the sacred are done with "religious" zeal.

Religion is man's tool for tapping the depth of spiritual life. Religion makes ultimate meaning and courage available to man. The tragic aspect of religion, however, is that it makes itself the ultimate and despises the secular realm.

> For the religious and the secular realm are in the same predicament. Neither of them should be in separation from the other, and both should realize that their very existence as separated is an emergency, that both of them are rooted in religion in the larger sense of the word, in the experience of ultimate concern. [18]

Tillich is ever ready to admit the tentative nature of religious rituals, practices, and institutions. Religion can become insensitive to its depth. It can become a means of escaping from the real world. The theologian's task is to clean out the religious filter so that the depth dimensions of life might be best appropriated. When the juices of understanding and creativity are freely flowing through the religious filters, then "religion is the substance of culture, culture is the form of religion." [19] Cultural forms and expressions are vital in carrying the freight of religious symbolism.

In sharp contrast to Bonhoeffer, Tillich maintains that only because of the "religious objectifications" of church traditions, rituals, sacramental activities, and the biblical message has the biblical faith been able to survive. In a similar vein Tillich runs counter to Barth in maintaining that the philosophical enterprise has helped to clarify the biblical understanding of what life is all about.

Tillich's insistence upon the need for the maintenance of religious formulations and institutions as fundamental to the human condition is qualified by his "Bonhoefferian" concern better known as the "Protestant Principle": Religious institutions are fallible and theological formulations are relative. In spite of the danger which religious stagnation or solidification poses in a fast-moving age, religious symbols and practices are vital to the human situation. Religious affirmations and symbols enable us to appropriate the contemporary demands and future possibilities of our society better than we can do so without them.

Without losing step the drumbeat is picked up by Meland and we march on. The religious dimensions of culture and the cultural expressions of religion which are heralded in Tillich become the "religious sensibilities" of which we have already spoken in Meland's contributions to this discussion.

> Religious sensibility . . . has to do with the response of wonder and sensitivity to what inheres in the human structure as an intimation of A-More-Than-Human-Reality, to which the human structure is related as creature to ground, and toward which it has instinctive outreaches.[20]

According to Meland, it is "natural" for man to realize that the limits of his life are grounded in that which transcends his existence.

One aspect of man's ability to know and participate in that which transcends him is his awareness of hope. We have heard much of late concerning the theology of hope. For Meland hope means man's ability to see beyond the present situation. Man's ability to hope is grounded in his ability to withdraw from a life situation and reflect upon it.

Meland considers the "anti-religion" crusade of the secularizers to be not only an attack upon explicit religious institutions and practices, but also a disavowal of sensitivities and human expectations which enhance the image of man and enrich his life. The rich heritage of the Judaeo-Christian tradition of myth and symbolism cannot be negated without seriously endangering Western culture's very fabric and vitality.[21]

In spite of the attempts to sabotage religious expressions or even their limited ability to bear witness to the deeper dimensions of reality, they are vital to man's life experience. If a reorientation of the religious vision of life is necessary, then let it come. But we shall never be free of the need for "religious sensibilities," according to Meland.

CONCLUDING REMARKS

The problems raised by the advocates of "religionless Christianity" are a particular thorn in the side of the "Eclipse of the Secular" position. Meland, Tillich, and Eliade are particularly vulnerable to the claim that modern man can do without religion because of their avowed defense of religious expressions of life. However, Bonhoeffer's man-come-of-age may not be as free of the sacred and mature in his relationship to the world as he thinks. The point at which Meland, Tillich, and Eliade direct a rather telling assault upon the proponents of "religionless Christianity" is in the importance of myth and ritual. The contributions of these two schools of thought may represent the necessary ingredients in contemporary theology.

Since the writing of his earlier book, Harvey Cox has now sounded the sacred note in this sacred-secular duet. Although he doesn't call for religious expression in exactly the same manner that the adherents of the "Eclipse of the Secular" position have, he has, nevertheless, celebrated the contemporary "renaissance of fantasy and festivity." [22] In response to criticism of *The Secular City* and in an openness toward the religious resurgence in our time, Cox has called for the closing of the gap in today's world between "the world-changers and the life-celebrators." [23] His call for the affirmation of revelry, ritual, and myth comes like fresh breezes blowing across the barren reaches of contemporary depression. "Religionless Christianity" may not be all that "religion-less"!

A depth analysis of the mythical portrayal of life which is so clearly visible in the biblical tradition and yet so imperfectly understood is manifestly needed. The writers of the Hebrew tradition were especially adept at lifting up and speaking to the human situation through myth and ritual. The question today is: How may we dramatize man's intangible strivings? How do we "tell the stories" which will excite the imagination and call the committed to action? What are the myths and rituals which will enable us to celebrate life in its depth as well as in its more festive dimensions?

From Tillich we have gathered that man is a symbol-maker and symbol-user. We dare not lose sight of this contribution. From Bonhoeffer we have been told that religious adherents frequently lose sight of their purpose and vocation. We cannot afford to close our ears to his analysis. There is some truth in the chant: "Up with the secular; down with religion." But that partial truth must be placed alongside of the call of Meland to maintain those religious sensitivities which ground us in the abundant life!

With qualifications we might agree with C. B. Armstrong, who relates the following:

> Religion may not always be Christian in the deepest sense. . . . But in its lower values it is still most needful. Its discipline of withdrawal, its rhythm of seasons covering each aspect of life as well as recalling each phase of redemption, its heritage of art, music, and inspired writings and formularies, its provision of spiritual opportunities, its witness to the world, and its consecration of so many activities of human service, make institutional Christianity indispensable.[24]

In spite of the threat of institutional stagnation which hangs over the religious enterprise like an ominous cloud, human response is primarily sustained by concrete institutional forms and deep-rooted religious traditions.

At the risk of sounding simplistic and possibly causing sensitive linguists such as Paul Van Buren to protest, we might affirm the quest for "God's religion." In the midst of political machinery, economic and technological realities, and social and personal dimensions, the preservation of religious traditions and symbols which interpret our cultural experience in depth must be maintained. A very crucial example is the agony, frequently referred to as a "spiritual crisis," of the American people caused by the strangling effect of their involvement in Southeast Asia plus their racial schizophrenia. It is by no means accidental that the contemporary unrest and agitation is referred to as a "spiritual problem." The diminishing supply of "spirit" in a so-called "Christian" nation must be sufficient cause for a stench nauseating to God's sensitive nostrils!

The real test of the process of secularization comes at the

point of the substance of the sacred. That there should be an occasional "eclipse" of the sacred is understandable. A few minor changes in the old religious machine can resolve such problems. What if, however, the contemporary "eclipse" lasts longer and is more effective than earlier lapses? What if there should ever be a "total eclipse" of the sacred? This thought threatens those in the "Total Sacrality" camp as well as those in many other camps because the total eclipse of the sacred equals the death of God.

5
The
Death
of the
Sacred

"At one point in history, God and the priests seemed to become superfluous, yet the world went on as before."

Eric Hoffer[1]

Jesus once observed: "When the Son of Man comes, will he find faith on earth?" There were times during the height of the debate concerning the death of God when persons must have been reminded of his musing. However, it wasn't the nation's most vocal atheist, Madalyn Murray O'Hair, who had people so nervous. No indeed! During the height of the sixties the cry that "God is dead!" came from the Protestant seminaries. Although persons became irate over Mrs. O'Hair, they at least could categorize her and dismiss her. But that men of God could make similar claims was more than the average parishioner could take.

Although most eminent theologians were quick to criticize and dismiss the contribution of the most recent "God is dead" theologians, the ferment which they caused cannot be easily forgotten. There is truth in the statement that we have traveled this route before. But the most recent emergence of theological atheism must be dealt with in terms of its uniqueness as well as its contribution to the ongoing theological debate.

Prior to the recent emergence of radicalism, the criticism of the church had been initiated by persons who were leaving the ranks of the faithful. But the debate of the sixties was carried on by persons *within* the church. One might say that the church experienced its own extreme "secularity." The invasion or presence of such a radical secularity, of doubt, of skepticism, and of a sense of the meaninglessness of religious language inside the church must be taken seriously.

In the fifties the church was shocked to discover that it had to get its feet wet in the world if it was to be faithful to its Lord. The death of God controversy added insult to injury by claiming that the central reality of the church's faith and tradition was of a questionable status at best. Regardless of whether or not one considers the radical theologians to have provided us with the best tools of getting at the "God" question, they have driven us to deal with the fundamental question of our faith — the nature and existence of God.

One might claim with some justification that the ground covered in the death of God controversy had been traversed before by such "heavyweights" as Feuerbach, Marx, and Nietzsche. Nevertheless, one cannot ignore the prophetic ring of Nietzsche's madman who declares: "I came too early; my time has not yet come. This dreadful occurrence is still on its way." [2] That there is nothing new about the announcement that "God is dead" is true, but the character of the messengers and the receptivity of their audience is different with each epoch. Whether the madman's pronouncement has finally been "heard" is still open for question.

We cannot understand the contemporary theological situation without considering the two giants of recent memory — Paul Tillich and Karl Barth. Both Barth and Tillich struggled with the Nietzschean cry, "God is dead!" The theology which Barth developed in response to Nietzsche was the God of Christian revelation who was as alive as his Word which still confounded man's estimate of himself and came to him with the offer of grace in Jesus Christ. Tillich, taking the opposite course, had claimed that the God of Christian revelation would continue to live to the extent that he was found in the awareness of a transcendent dimension of the world latent in human consciousness. Both Tillich and Barth were concerned to prove that God was not really dead, but dead only in a false image of deity held by the impious or the ignorant. Each theologian claimed that an imposter, called by the name of God, has been laid in the grave, while the true God lives still.

The death of God theology of the sixties arose out of dissatisfaction with these two answers. To Barth the claim was made that hope can be based upon human effort. To Tillich the claim was made that life need not be a shallow, meaningless affair even without the hope that lay in the sense of the eternal glimpsed beyond the temporal. The radical theologians posed a particularly significant challenge for the Barthian position. If one begins with the category of God's transcendence and proceeds to support a religionless Christianity, then one may end up with a God so heavenly that he is no "earthly good"!

Langdon Gilkey, in his book *Naming the Whirlwind,* spells out several major assertions of neoorthodox theology against which radical theologians have most recently reacted: 1) the reality, the sovereignty, and the all-sufficiency of God relates to his creation, especially to mankind and his troubled history, and the consequent need on the part of man for God; 2) corresponding lostness, estrangement, helplessness, and sinfulness characterize man and his works; 3) man is absolutely dependent for both truth and grace on the special revelation of God in the lives of the Hebrew people and especially through Jesus Christ; 4) the knowledge gained by the ordinary disciplines of science or of historiography can at best be only supplementary to Christian theology; 5) the content of faith was demonstrable and knowable only if one possessed faith; and, 6) faith was the necessary precondition for works of love.[3]

As Hamilton and van Buren remind us, this theology at the end claimed to know too much. A vision that had begun with a sense of the almost impenetrable mystery of life amidst loss and despair, ended as a system of dogmas asserted with apodictic certainty and vast overconfidence; like a good political administration that had been in power too long, it was ripe for a fall.[4]

The emergence of radical theologians was a reaction to

what they considered to be the meaningless nature of the God-language of neoorthodox theology. The silence of the sixties was soon broken by the cry of Nietzsche's madman once more, "God is dead!" The difference between making the pronouncement in the nineteenth century and in the middle of the twentieth century became obvious at least as far as coverage is concerned. The manner in which the press and news media picked up the slogan led adherents to refer to the early stages of their theological journey as the "journalistic stage." Even *Time* magazine in its Easter epistle of 1966 posed the question, "Is God Dead?" *The New Yorker* magazine sent Ved Mehta in quest of the "new" theologian who was bold enough to lay claim to God's death. Radical theology's greatest strength during its first phase was its ability to attract the mass media and to become known throughout the world by television and magazines.

"What sense did it make?" asks a public which is accustomed to thinking of seminary professors as the custodians, not as the destroyers, of their traditions! Although more has been made of the death of God movement than even its adherents were able to explain, this phase in theology is important for us to consider because it provides a link between the past and the future of the theological enterprise. Radical theology may have come the closest to expressing the secular mind of modern religious and Christian man in the second half of the twentieth century. It has also driven our theological attention to the primary rather than the secondary theological problems of our age. As one of the "near" radicals has said, "What this age is suffering from *primarily* is not a crisis of authority but a crisis of faith. Not that faith has slackened — it has been inflated. An inflationary faith typifies the crisis of this age." [5]

THE SECULAR

> "The rebel is a man who is on the point of accepting or rejecting the sacred and determined on laying claim to a human situation in which all the answers are human."   Camus[6]

In contrast to Harvey Cox, who has been intent upon the celebration of the secular, the two main adherents of the death of God school, William Hamilton and Thomas Altizer, have been more concerned with the dismissal of the sacred. They have not been insensitive to the contemporary expression of the secular world as it addressed the Christian tradition, however. They questioned the very symbol of God — what is meant by God if one cannot demonstrate God's being or his effects? What is meant by God if one cannot verify the word? As biblical theologians they shuddered as much as did the liberals or the secularists when Cecil B. DeMille's camera showed the Israelites walking through the Red Sea between walls of water and staring at the fish! No, said they, God acts in history, but not *that* way. Hamilton claimed that God not only does not act that way, but that he has not been experienced acting recently, *period!* To this Altizer joined in by claiming that it was in God's nature to pour himself into secular history in the Incarnation event and thus die on behalf of mankind.

In many ways I feel that the death of God movement is like a cadaver which has been viewed and previewed almost beyond recognition. What is there left to say? But because it may be helpful to place this theological expression within the larger context of contemporary thinking, we will deal briefly with the contributions of several of the death of God theologians.

Although Gabriel Vahanian is not considered one of the "hard" radicals, he was one of the earliest spokesmen for the idea of the death of God in the sixties. In his book entitled *The Death of God,* Vahanian began the exploration of the theme which was to capture the imagination of many a theological upstart before the decade was completed. One of his contributions in this book was the observation that the Christian faith has usually provided a place for man's faithlessness, that faith in God was somehow bound up in man's faithlessness: "Lord, I believe; help thou mine unbelief." But, according to Vahanian, it now appears that the Christian faith has ceased to provide for unbelief. As a result, contact with modern man has been lost. "In the present age doubt has become immune to faith and faith has dissociated itself from doubt. Nothing is worse than a dead faith, except a dead doubt." [7]

As one recalls the role which doubt plays in the biblical

experience, the thought of Vahanian takes on meaning for us. He goes on to point out that modern man is the legatee of the Christian as well as the atheist. He agrees with the Christian that all depends upon grace. He agrees with the atheist that God is dead. This ambiguity between grace and doubt is the context of contemporary man, according to Vahanian. "But God's absence, or the death of God itself, has become what a man directly experiences. It is no longer a theoretical declaration; it is a practical awareness by which authentic existence often is measured." [8]

It was as if Vahanian were preparing the way for those "who were to come"! That is, Vahanian recognized the difficulty of being a man of faith in the last half of the twentieth century. He recognized that the Christian faith had allowed itself to be "boxed in"; that is, the Christian faith had not allowed enough of the experience of secularity to be a part of its experience. This absence of doubt has led contemporary man to experience the death of God, according to Vahanian.

Standing in the wings and seemingly waiting for this cue was Thomas Altizer, along with William Hamilton, the two major proponents of the death of God movement in the sixties. In order to arrive at the conclusion that God was to be listed among the deceased, Altizer relied upon the thought of Eliade along with some poetic literature. Altizer understood that God or the sacred denied its own existence in order to become incarnate in the reality of the secular — the world. In theological parlance this is known as a radical *kenosis* — God pouring himself out into history and life. According to Altizer this "pouring out" took place in the Christ event; thus we live in the age of the death of God.

For Altizer the thrust of the Incarnation in Christian theology is that God has compromised or negated himself in order to become incarnate in the world process. This theme is akin to the teaching in the Gospel of John about the preexistent Christ who denied himself this heavenly existence in order to become man. Altizer interprets this to be the climactic event of a continual process of God's pouring himself into history. This process eventually leads to the elimination of the sacred.[9] What is the secular? It's merely what's left when we accept the death of the transcendent. The secular is not only the created order secularized by the God who transcends it (the Barthians), but the secular is all that there is.

Altizer feels that he was able to find clues to this cosmic event within the literature of the Western world. He was able to see in the ecstatic urgings of the poet Blake or the philosophical rantings of a Nietzsche the legitimation of the belief that the death of God was upon us.

Although Paul Van Buren should not be seen as portraying the same message as Altizer, he does provide an important link within the broader framework of secular theology. Van Buren was primarily concerned with the content of the faith language as such. Was it intelligible to modern man? Could faith language be tested empirically? In fact, was it possible to set forth a "secular" interpretation of the gospel?

Van Buren began with the question raised by Bonhoeffer, "How can the Christian who is himself a secular man understand his faith in a secular way?" [10] Van Buren contends that the gospel must be made meaningful for the thinking man of industry and science who is pragmatic and empirical. Van Buren parts company with the Bonhoefferians in that he doesn't conceive the battle to be focused upon the nature of religion and the confusion between religion and Christian faith, but rather that the difficulty lies in the character of the language of faith.[11] It does not make sense to Van Buren for him to continue Bonhoeffer's search for a "nonreligious" interpretation of biblical concepts while continuing to speak of God. Van Buren is in fact reticent to speak of God "in himself."

Van Buren represents a direct challenge to the "secularity" of Bonhoeffer or Gogarten Some claim that Van Buren is attempting to jettison the sacred *in toto*. He not only would deny any limit to the secularization of the world process but would seemingly even accept a total secularization of the faith itself. Van Buren represents a peculiar challenge to the theological enterprise because he has equated the "secular" with that which is verifiable in experience. As a language analyst he is concerned to see whether theological vocabulary is verifiable or meaningful when put through the same wringer through which all language must go to be considered meaningful.

Thus we find these two quite divergent opinions within what has become known as the death of God movement. Altizer the mystic points out that the content of human experience is that of God's death. Van Buren the linguist maintains that the Christian vocabulary cannot be exempted from a rigorous analysis in the secular arena.

SECULARITY

T. S. Eliot's "The Rock" quite appropriately describes the situation which the death of God theologians claim is upon us:

> But it seems that something has happened that has never happened
>   before: though we know not just when, or why, or how, or where.
> Men have left GOD not for other gods, they say, but for no god; and
>   this has never happened before.
> That men both deny gods and worship gods, professing first Reason,
> And then Money, and Power, and what they call Life, or Race, or
>   Dialectic.
> The Church disowned, the tower overthrown, the bells upturned,
>   what have we to do
> But stand with empty hands and palms turned upwards
> In an age which advances progressively backwards?[12]

Going beyond Eliot, Altizer has claimed that it is in the nature of God to have denied himself existence so that man might experience manhood. In the words of Hamilton the death of God calls for the affirmation of radical freedom on the part of man. This new manhood is not, in the words of Eliot, advancement into the past, however.

Is there a peculiarly secular mood to which the radical theologians have been most sensitive? Is modern man incapable of ordering his life in terms of transcendence? Martin Buber, some two decades ago, reacted to the proclamation of God's death by maintaining that such a claim is an admission that man has become incapable of apprehending a reality absolutely independent of himself and of having a relation with it.[13] But Buber called this experience or lack of experience of God "the eclipse of God" and not a sign of his death. Man was just not "tuned in" appropriately to the transcendent.

The death of God theologians have claimed, on the other hand, that man not only does not relate meaningfully to transcendence but his experience is of "death" when he does experience God. Peter Berger sized up the ambiguity of this experience or lack of experience of transcendence by saying, "The departure of the supernatural has been received in a variety of moods — with prophetic anger, in deep sorrow, with gleeful triumph, or simply as an emotionally unprovocative fact." [14] The reception given this "event" by the proponents of this movement varies. Altizer claims that the Christian without God is a waiting man who dares to descend into the darkness, grappling with all that is profane in order to claim it on man's behalf. The Christian without God for Van Buren is Jesus' man, perfectly free, lord of all, subject to none. Hamilton seems to hold both of these dimensions of the experience of the death of God in tension. He recognizes the agony of the deterioration of the God-man relationship but celebrates the freedom of man to live within the profane context of the contemporary world.

Martin Marty is not very generous in his compliments to this theological understanding. The claiming of the support of the secular man as a clean, cool ally to help people rid themselves of false God-talk is one thing. But to allow oneself the luxury of staying within the Christian camp while speaking of the death of God is a gymnastic maneuver which Marty finds hard to follow. But if Van Buren, Hamilton, and Altizer were to leave Protestant soil, they would have great difficulty in claiming Jesus as hero. "Secular man" would still have to claim Jesus "as author and finisher of faith, as exemplar and enactor of freedom, as agent of desacralization in nature and of secularization in history, as critic of religion, as first fruit of the new creation, first citizen of 'the secular city.'" [15]

If we recognize with Van Buren, for example, that contemporary man no longer looks to some transcendent being for life's primary purpose, if we recognize that he no longer expects some divine power to change the course of history from outside of history, will he still be receptive to a gospel which is secular, or otherwise? Van Buren assumes that life is self-explanatory so that the Christian tradition must be reinterpreted to allow the secular mind to interpret its claims. For Van Buren then, we must present the possibility of "keeping the faith" apart from a view of the world which includes a transcendent reference — thus without God. Van Buren has thus given us a "secular" meaning of the gospel. Like Bultmann, he has acted out of the conviction that the world view in which the gospel is couched is unintelligible to contemporary man. A gospel without God may sound weird to most of us, but it indicates the extent to which some contemporary theologians are willing to go in order to speak a relevant word to our world.

What if Van Buren is right in his assessment of what needs to be done theologically? What if he is correct in saying that what is called for is a gospel without transcendent trappings? Will such a gospel be received? Marty, with a sense of earthiness or cynicism, points out that a board chairman of a large firm will doubtless feel threatened by the death of God theologian, an advocate of the secular city or radical theology. He will return anxiously to the symbols which sustained and propelled our society ahead, because these traditional symbols are identified with the capitalistic system which has been his ladder to success.

The contemporary businessman may well be embarrassed by Wesleyan evangelicalism, and he may not read the Bible to learn how to run his business anymore, but he will not repudiate it or demythologize it; he will probably subsidize the clergyman who will keep on reassuring him that his way of doing business is God's way.[16]

Therefore, if Van Buren is right about the need to reach secular man, he is very mistaken in thinking that a "secular" word will be accepted in the place of traditional religious language. We may have to wait for the emergence of a truly secular consciousness which will be able to respond to a secular gospel.

Langdon Gilkey maintains, however, that the spirit, mood, or mind of our contemporary culture is secular. Whether that means that 99.44 percent of the population is incapable of experiencing the transcendent or claiming the same is still open for discussion. How contemporary man reacts to the secular spirit which pervades his life is not yet determinable. That the radical theologians understand the presence of the secular spirit as symptomatic of an existence which is devoid of the divine, and thus affirming the death of God, is painfully clear.

Langmead Casserley maintains that there is an alternative

way of interpreting the presence of the secular spirit or mentality of our time. He claims that the state of being "without God" is the normal condition of man: "Being 'without God' provides no reason at all for denying the divine existence." [17] According to Casserley, it is not the absence of God which disturbs us but rather its interpretation. He cites a familiar jingle to illustrate his point:

> Yesterday upon the stair
> I met a man who wasn't there.
> He wasn't there again today
> I wish to God he'd go away.[18]

For Casserley the experience of the reality of God as that of the man who isn't there is not unique with this generation. "God is experienced today above all as the absent one who ought to be there, and indeed whose absence seems well nigh scandalous and intolerable." [19] The options about what kind of God is absent are there for anyone to claim. This "absence" can be experienced as the God of Abraham, Isaac, and Jacob, or this "absence" can be a sign of God's death or nonexistence, according to Casserley. We shall return to this theme of the absence of God in the last chapter.

Hamilton's response to Casserley is simply, "We are not talking about the absence of the experience of God, but about the experience of the absence of God." [20] In effect, Hamilton is asking us to frankly admit that God is not there, that he is dead, rather than to go on talking about a God who is never present in our experience and whose absence we feel so strongly. Holden Caulfield, in J.D. Salinger's *The Catcher in the Rye,* reflects some of the same call for honesty as he is reacting to the "sermonic voice" of preachers. He asks why they cannot use their "natural voice." [21] Now Hamilton and the other secular theologians have dared to put aside their sermonic voices in order to speak in a natural voice about their experience of life and of God. Such frankness has been shocking to many people, but it has opened up what is perhaps the most significant issue for theology in the last part of the twentieth century. We have yet to see whether this same honesty about the experience of God can be shared by others in our time. Can we deal with the experience of the absence of God?

THE PROCESS OF SECULARIZATION

If God is dead and no longer at work in history, as the radical theologians claim, what led them to this conclusion? The factors which have contributed to the secular mentality of our contemporary society have also contributed to the irrelevance of God for certain individuals. There are at least three general areas upon which the sources of radical Christianity are based. We have already made mention of the use made of nineteenth-century writers such as Blake and Nietzsche. The influence of Nietzsche's "madman" is seen most clearly in the writings of Altizer and Hamilton.

Paul Van Buren has become convinced of the need for a secular interpretation of the Christian witness because of pragmatic and empirical thinking at work in industry and science which has so shaped the context of the human situation that it is meaningless to live any more with the God hypothesis. He contends that because this empirical mentality is so pervasive even the gospel must be interpreted after a secular fashion.

The third area which has been referred to by the radical theologians and especially Altizer is the doctrine of the Incarnation. In the Christ event Altizer claims that God has poured himself into history. This leaves man to be responsible for his own destiny.

To understand the process of secularization in the context of these factors is to see it not only as the proper place for the man of faith according to Gogarten and Bonhoeffer, but even more as the total movement of history away from a transcendent explanation of life. The process of secularization not only calls for the death of God but also the affirmation that man is now totally responsible for his world.

The Barthians were willing to baptize the process of secularization as God's will but they were not as willing to see the process turned on their understanding of God. The radical theologians, on the other hand, have claimed that secularization forces drastic changes upon theology itself. The inherited biblical faith is rendered as irrelevant and empty. Van Buren has been especially quick to recognize that the secular spirit we all share tends to be subversive of any sort of faith and discourse that might be called authentically biblical.

Gilkey points out that the biblical faith is not the only casualty in the process of secularization.

> . . . *all* the gods are dead — that is, all ultimate structures of co-herence, order, and value in the wider environment of man's life have vanished; and, finally, that symbolic or religious speech, referent to a dimension of mystery beyond the evident and the sensible, is also dead.[22]

Many of us can accept as a well-established fact that we will never be able to speak of God in the old way. But is it too much to hope that the experience of wholeness will be visited upon us once again? Vahanian sees a real danger in this situation if we have "domesticated the universe" and lost the cipher of its symbols as well. This fear is an echo of the theme found so often in Meland and Tillich.

Thus the most recent claim that God's death is upon us is not an isolated event. It stands at the end (or middle) of a long history in Western thought. The spirit set forth by a Darwin or a Nietzsche, a Russell or a Freud, is a determining factor in any theological enterprise today. Their shadow is cast upon any contemporary theological effort. The proclamation of the death of God has a religious and philosophical heritage of three hundred years of Western thought from Copernicus to Nietzsche. We have moved beyond the tendency to "outflank" or "attack" God to an almost humble acceptance of his death. Whether this process of secularization has been properly understood by Altizer and Hamilton is obviously debatable. That it has become *the* agenda for the next decade is becoming increasingly obvious. Put simply, we've all got a "God problem"!

RELIGION AND CHRISTIANITY

> "Only, where are they? the flowers, the familiar, the crowns of the feast-day?
> . . . Why no more does a god mark a mortal man's forehead . . ."
> Friedrich Holderlin, *Bread and Wine*[22]

It was only a matter of time before followers of Barth would escalate the transcendent out of sight. It was to be expected that the warnings of a Kierkegaard or a Bonhoeffer concerning religion would come to include religion's God as well. The stress which Barth placed upon the utter transcendence of God provided the groundwork for those who would affirm that the lack of evidence of the involvement of God in the historical process indicates that the "Transcendent One" has totally abdicated. This assumption has become, for Hamilton especially, the conclusion of the Barthian affirmation.

The point at which Altizer, Hamilton, and Van Buren differ radically from the thrust of "religionless Christianity" is that they dismiss the God of Christianity but keep its religion. These three theologians have attempted in varying degrees to preserve the historical and ethical dimension of the Judaeo-Christian tradition along with certain aspects of the theological tradition. Since the traditional "God concept" is linked with a unifying principle or absolute, and since for them such a view is no longer tenable, all vestiges of the "God concept" must go.

We have previously noted that Van Buren has been warning us that advocates of the Christian faith must become more cautious in their use of language concerning God. Contemporary culture, according to Van Buren, indicates that there are many ways of looking and seeing, many points of orientation, and that attempts to pull these together into one grand scheme do not bring us closer to understanding how things are. The term "God" for Van Buren has ceased to be a meaningful term around which man can organize the contemporary culture. Man cannot resort to use of this transcendent absolute in interpreting the many expressions of human existence which confront him. Man is totally responsible for the ordering of the world.

From the perspective of total "secularity" theological language is frequently meaningless and, indeed, God as a force in the universe is dead. Contemporary critics attack Van Buren for his preservation of the Christ of Christianity while dispensing with the God of faith. Is it possible to maintain the Jesus of Nazareth as the truly free man and call for commitment to him without the God to whom that Jesus related as a transcendent being? That most difficult of questions has not been satisfactorily dealt with by either Van Buren or Hamilton. The historical freedom which many feel to be a part of the life and witness of Jesus is of a fragile order. Its persistence among secular humanity may be more difficult to keep alive than man-on-his-own is able to maintain.

Van Buren's efforts touched upon a sensitive nerve-ending in the thought of Langdon Gilkey for he calls Van Buren's evaluation of the language of faith "linguistic madness." Gilkey relates that, "Van Buren thus seems to wish to have his cake and eat it too, to wish to be a radical innovator, and yet to be 'orthodox.'" [24] Gilkey also considers Van Buren's empirical Christianity to be an attempt to "interpret the Christian gospel in about as radically different a way as is imaginable, namely without God." [25]

Whether or not we are convinced by Van Buren's efforts, he appears to be rightfully struggling with the meaning of the Christian faith for contemporary man. Our judgments must be a bit more reserved as we "wait and see" if Van Buren is not able to make a valuable contribution to the intense problem of communication. Communication of the deposit of faith must be central in the church's agenda in the coming years.

A final critical comment is in order, however, not at the point of Van Buren's refusal to speak of God, but in regard to his quite limited tools to deal with the communication problem. Is man basically an empirical being? Granted that the world of science and technology bears in upon the contemporary man, is his nature exhausted by that world dimension? Or is the empirical dimension one among several which helps us to understand the current crisis for the man of faith? Who is man and what is his mentality? This problem continues with us as we proceed with this study.

The nature of the current crisis of faith is a difficult phenomenon to get a grip on. We have referred to studies and opinion polls which tell us that God, or at least belief in the same, has never been more alive. Those who claim that we are on the verge of not only religionless Christianity but a God-less Christianity may be more prophetic than empirically accurate. But with the radicals we must ask the question, "What kind of faith is still strong in the lives of the 'average' American?" Can the religious resurgence of the fifties be seen as just another in a series of Christian capitulations? As Vahanian relates:

Christianity is today synonymous with religiosity. Its appeal to the masses is based on a diluted version of the original faith. The gap between the gospel and "the power of positive thinking" is greater than the one which, according to Tertullian (c. 160-220 A.D.), separated Athens from Jerusalem — pagan wisdom from Biblical truth.[26]

Thus we might well say that the radical theologians may be, for all practical purposes, correct in their analysis of the contemporary religious climate. But their pronouncement for the most part has fallen on deaf ears because popular theology operates on a different wave length. As Vahanian has said so well, the pronouncement by the Hollywood actress turned Sunday school teacher, "God is a livin' doll," is a more damning pronouncement than Nietzsche's decree of the death of God.

In Samuel Beckett's *Waiting for Godot* there is a priceless line by Estragon when he is asked whether he remembers the Gospels:

> I remember the maps of the Holy Land. Coloured they were. Very pretty. The Dead Sea was pale blue. The very look of it made me thirsty. That's where we'll go, I used to say, that's where we'll go for our honeymoon. We'll swim. We'll be happy.[27]

Estragon is probably a more accurate portrayal of contemporary American religiosity than is Nietzsche's madman. For that reason we may have to continue to wait for the death of Him who has been pronounced dead so frequently. Nietzsche's phrase that our culture has "murdered him" is a half truth. We've done a poor job of it!

CONCLUDING REMARKS

"The report of my death," wrote Mark Twain to a newspaper that was somewhat premature with his obituary notice, "has been greatly exaggerated!" Is it possible that the so-called "death of God" theologians have been guilty of a similar journalistic "exaggeration"? One thing is obvious, namely that the particular furor over God's demise which erupted in the sixties has subsided. A recent *Time* magazine religion section article began with the question, "Is 'God Is Dead' Dead?" It mentioned, for example, that Thomas Altizer is quietly teaching English on Long Island. Does it mean that the most recent death of God scandal was just another flash in the theological frying pan? Does it mean with

Nietzsche that the time for God's demise has *still* not yet come? Was the discussion concerning God's demise more accurately the death of neoorthodoxy? Waiting for answers to these questions may be as time consuming as "waiting for Godot"!

However, we must admit that the death of God movement made many of us nervous. We are just not that firmly convinced of his existence. Perhaps the proclamation of the sixties missed the mark as far as accuracy is concerned, but the question of God's existence caught most theologians in the crossfire. Whether the future of theology deals with God's death or his life, it will not be able to avoid many of the nitty-gritty problems raised by Altizer, Hamilton, and Van Buren.

Some of us may have "talked with God this morning!" Some of us may be singing "God is alive and well!" But others of us are not resting quite so easily. A recent bumper sticker put it, "If your God is dead, try mine!" We may have to go on trying for some time before we gain a perspective on the God problem which will provide us with a theological basis for our faith stance. The word "God" needs to be spoken in new and refreshing ways before we will reach the end of the tunnel through which we are presently passing.

Participants in the death of God movement have discerned and expressed in their thought the anatomy of the present situation. But their critics have raised the question whether they have provided us with a viable interpretation of the Christian faith or a valid symbolic account of our general human experience, secular or otherwise.

Radical theology has pointed up the weakness of faith and illustrated what is for increasing numbers of persons the experience of the absence of God. It has called into question theological understanding based on revelation or on metaphysical inquiry. With theological giants like Barth and Tillich standing in the wings we witnessed the center stage performance of the radical theologians. With Cooper we may well conclude: "It has not been the great yea-sayers alone, but the yea-sayers in concert with the equally great nay-sayers of history, who have built up Western Christian theology and Western culture in general." [28]

Radical theology will speak to us to the extent that we

become aware of the levels of uneasiness and doubt pressing in upon each of us in our theological journey. Death of God theology is not dead. Many of us may wish that it would die and go away, but apparently it will not. It will not go away because it is symbolic of the problems and needs of our historical period in a far more important way than it is significant as a philosophical or theological movement.

A final comment about the "radical" theologians is that they weren't "radical" enough. Theology must be radical not only in its rhetoric but also in its political thrust and human consequences. The agenda which the radical theologians forced upon us is the discovery of transcendence. In the next chapter we will be searching for ways of locating transcendence in the midst of political-historical reality. It may be that in the death and rebirth of Western theological thinking new theological alternatives may emerge. This death and rebirth must come in thought as well as in *praxis*, in politics and in the struggle of the powerless to become the authors of history rather than its footnotes.

The death of God movement has opened for us not only the possibilities of theological reflection but the Pandora's box of faithless doubt as well. The theological lid will never fit as tightly again. We stand in many ways with the helpless and disoriented Mary Magdalene, weeping outside Jesus' apparently empty tomb, "because they have taken away my Lord." We must set ourselves to the task of recovering the presence or accepting the absence of God.

6
The
Sacred
Through
the Secular

Critics may be correct in saying that the death of God movement did not provide us with any alternatives for a healthy theological future. It may also be premature to proclaim that the contemporary faith experience is that of God's death. However, we also have been reminded that religious language was in need of some overhauling. Furthermore, we knew deep down that Tillich and Barth would not live forever. Even so, those in the death of God movement have seemed to many like mischievous schoolboys with erasers in hand wiping clean the theological chalkboards of their precious writ! We find it very difficult to find the way to our theological destination when we are not even sure what is to be the correct starting point.

In the church we are living on the other side of the event forecast in the play *Green Pastures*. God is discussing the forthcoming flood with Noah as he says, "De levees gonter bust an' everything dat's fastened down is comin' loose." We are theologically living after the flood. Familiarities have been destroyed like trailer houses in the path of a hurricane.

Whether we have proclaimed God's death, are "waiting

without idols," or for Godot, or have ceased waiting alto-
gether, we shall in the following paragraphs explore some of
the theological dimensions of the problems of faith in the
waning years of the twentieth century. Together we will
attempt to discover whether there are available categories of
meaning which will support us and opportunities to serve
which sufficiently sustain our spirits.

In many ways the secular theologians only began the
grueling task of formulating a "worldly" theology. If the liberal
theology of the early decades of this century was the thesis in
a Hegelian thesis-antithesis-synthesis schema and the neoorthodox tradition was the antithesis, then a worldly theology
may become the new synthesis. This may mean that the
function of radical theology was that of negation. Its protests
and its affirmations may well, however, set the stage for
relevant theological discussion today. With the radical theologians we affirm that the present stage is characterized by
discontinuity. The theological context may continue to be
like a street disorder in the midst of which we are called to
get our "theological selves together."

The theological radicals of recent years have appropriately
pointed out the tenuous nature of the theological enterprise.
But going beyond them we are called to be radicals of another
sort. We are called to be radical in the sense that we are
willing to plumb to the depths of human experience and enter
into the struggles for justice and freedom which are erupting
at so many levels of our society. As men of faith we are called
to press to the bottom of our theological constructs to discover
whether they still are able to enliven our spirits and motivate
us to enter into the decision-making processes which are shaping our destinies and the lives of countless persons who are
thus prevented from becoming fully human. As people of
God we need to hear again the "reveille for radicals" which
will call us to develop those theological tools best equipped
to aid in the development of a more human and just society.

A theology and life-style which takes the world more seriously than the "Sacred Against the Secular" stance but is hopefully better able to re-create a viable faith for the future
than was accomplished by the radical theologians is our
projected aim.

THE SECULAR

One of the exhibits at the world exposition in Montreal which picked up the theme "Man and His World" portrayed the detailed cosmology held by the early church. It included the enumeration of the various levels of the world with Jerusalem and Rome at the center of the world, purgatory somewhere south of the southern hemisphere, and sufficient categories of the afterlife in between to contain persons of various levels of disrepute. Living in such a world left little to the imagination if one believed in the established world view. If you were a "prevaricating judge," you would eventually end up in the eighth layer of the underworld writhing in boiling wax. Theological schismatics would eventually find themselves somewhat closer in proximity to the likes of Cain, Judas, and Lucifer! That was a very clear understanding of the world.

Not only are we presently less sure of "that" world beyond, but we are not at all convinced of the nature of "this" one and of our place in it. We have come a long way from the early church in the intervening centuries. We have increasingly moved from God's world to man's. Regions of life previously thought to be part of the eternal order are being increasingly brought under the scrutiny and control of man, if not completely, at least "for all practical purposes." The historical sieve which we have called secularization has gradually sifted out increasing numbers of religious hypotheses and called for their critical reevaluation. Few religious images have escaped this process.

Not only have men of faith discovered that their religious faith has had rather rough treatment but increasingly the spirit of the times is that of relentless protest against fixed norms. The results of scientific research and historical inquiry have uncovered the relativity and therefore possibly the implausibility of the sacred interpretation of things. The people of faith who have been insensitive to this process and have attempted to maintain a defensive sacred colonialism with respect to the world have allowed the "field of operation" of God in history to be repeatedly reduced in scope.

Previous generations of men have been better able to

establish principles, discern structures, and evaluate forces and events from a certain elevated position above the confusion of daily existence. But the awesome power of the penetrating forces of our day have demolished man's traditional focal points. Joseph Sittler has used an interesting play on words to refer to the phenomenon. The phrase, which was posed for him by a student, was, "How can *anything* mean if *everything* doesn't?" All facts, things, and thoughts exist in a relationship where it is no longer possible to order one's reflection from some secure position and to regard things from a single perspective. The orbit of the possible has been vastly enlarged. Attempts which we make to fix, place, and think in an organized fashion about anything may be doomed to failure or frustration at the least. As Gilkey relates,

> Where are the ultimate events of revelation when all in history swims in the relativity of time; what is the Word of God amidst the welter and variety of historical words in scripture; what is the mind of the Church in this manifold of changing historical minds . . . ?[1]

This recognition of the time-bound nature of so much of our tradition is also expressed in the heightened sensitivity toward what we refer to as the generation gap. The increasingly volatile and critical nature of some of today's youth points up the secular spirit which pervades our age. No authority is above question. This scrutiny is illustrative of what Munby points out about a secular society: "A secular society deflates the pretensions of politicians, but also the pretensions of judges, who vainly attempt to preserve some relics of their former role as prophet-priests of the national conscience."[2]

One can easily recognize that while youth are rejecting or calling into question forms of leadership, economic structures, and moral codes of behavior, they are also developing styles of dress or living which demonstrate their discontent. One might say that this is in part due to the absence of clearly defined images or guidelines for a human life-style. James Luther Adams refers to these ideal conceptions of man as "anthropological forms." In the history of man this ideal has ranged all the way from ascetic to thinker, to saint, to gentleman, to martyr. Most recently, Harvey Cox has called for a recovery of man the celebrator or jester.

Models are presently needed to enable persons to be human in our technological society. We are provided with the image of man as "master of his own fate" yet not sure that he is really in control of what is happening around him or has found a secure place in the structure of society. Thus we find ourselves in a society where some people are over-institutionalized and others are institutionless. The polarities of this experience are grounded, on the one hand, in the corporate structures and large educational structures, and, on the other hand, in the absence of institutional structures in our urban centers.

Just as it is increasingly difficult to sort out an appropriate image or pattern for one's life, so, too, the theologian is challenged to discover the structure within which theological symbols and patterns of behavior are still meaningful. The tendency of our scientific-technological society to develop a functional orientation toward life forces the man of faith to try to build an all-encompassing world view which might suit our pragmatic age.

If we are correct in maintaining that there is no secular realm as opposed to a sacred realm, then we must wrestle with the fact that many traditional theological symbols (not the least of which is "God") need some remodeling work. The problem of the secular has arisen and continues to arise when the sacred order of things has been unable to cope with and exhaust the meaning of the total world situation. The realm of the secular refers to those areas of life which cannot be accounted for in our religious world view. As aspects of our theology become "frozen" or arthritic with age, then we may no longer be able to account for contemporary life. As one fellow cleric proclaimed concerning the youthful rebelliousness of the times and his failure to comprehend it, "Life seems to be passing me by!" As a man of faith, certain aspects of life had become secular. That is, he could no longer interpret them theologically. We must now be willing to risk our religious heritage in the midst of the marketplace or it will become obsolete. To be men of faith patterned after the style of life of one Jesus of Nazareth, we must allow the total world situation to be our teacher and to shape our humanity.

The task of the theologian or man of faith is to continually point up the inadequacy of previous symbols and church postures, and to be sensitive to the way in which these symbols and patterns of life need to be reevaluated so that they might continue to evoke the most adequate response possible in a day which is not particularly conducive to prophetic religion. Our theological world view is secular in the sense that it is relative to the changing cultural scene. On the other hand, our symbols, rituals, creeds, and patterns of church life are sacred to the extent that they continue to enable us to deal meaningfully with this world. The real test of our religious traditions is their ability to function meaningfully for successive generations of the faithful.

One of the peculiar yet critical challenges to the contemporary American churchman is the recognition and acceptance of the fact that the Constantinian Age is over. The church is no longer able to assume comfortably that it is meaningfully shaping the contemporary American scene. The American church has not suffered from the development of the scientific-technological order to any great extent because it has uncritically internalized the values which make the system work. The real threat to the American church is not that it is flirting with a secular theology but that it too frequently and uncritically reflects the values and moods of the political, economic, and social situation. For this reason the contemporary religious scene has not become eroded by the times in the manner of its European and English counterparts. The American church has grown comfortable in its surroundings. The real challenge to the American church is to develop a faithful body of believers who are secular in their worldly wisdom and sacred in their disciplined adherence to the demands of the faith.

The disturbing paradox is that modern Christians are in fact more secular in their lives than their statements of faith would indicate. We must conclude that the affirmations of faith are not what primarily inform personal and social behavior. This disparity must be pointed up and critically analyzed. On the other hand, the so-called secular man may exist in significantly different terms than are indicated by the secular symbols through which he understands his existence.

Meanwhile, the world will not keep silent when we enter the

holy temple. The world writhes in anguish and flails its children violently about. Nevertheless, we are called to embrace the world. We must be about the task of understanding the world and filling it with meaning. To embrace the world means that we do not do so with many of the previous claims to authority. The terms upon which we enter the arena are worldly terms — political terms. Worldly theology is political theology! To take the world more seriously today means taking the political nature of ourselves and our faith more seriously. This stance does not mean calling for a new Constantinian consensus which reflects and gives credence to popular moods or political pronouncements.

To develop a political theology means to recognize that our every move in life is political. Our lives are shaped by a multitude of decision-making structures. To create new life and to instill the old with vigor means to enter into the life process as men of faith and change things. To take the world seriously is to address the issues of air pollution, war, draft resistance, or racial crisis. It means that one seeks political alternatives which will be more responsive to people in the streets. We may become actively involved in the development of community organizations which enable persons to achieve some sense of dignity and power. Whether we become actively involved in a political campaign, begin to deal with less-desirable youth, raise serious questions about police practices, or take up a free and critical style in any number of ways, we need to be clear about our goals and our motives. In other words, we cannot make a missional move of any consequence today without being political. Once we enter the political arena the theological footing provided by our ancestors becomes treacherous at best.

We need to develop a political theology. To the extent that we develop such a style of thinking and acting we will have moved beyond the impasse of the death of God movement. Ours will be a theology which is more radical to the extent that it is more serious about the world.

SECULARITY

"He alone is modern who is fully conscious of the present."

Jung[3]

Secularity has a relative meaning depending upon one's

understanding of the faith and the world. Because those in the "Sacred Against the Secular" group wish to maintain the purity of the Christian way of thinking, they are threatened by the secular world. The "Sacred-Secular Paradox" position celebrates the coming of the secular mentality because it is the outgrowth of what God is doing in his world. It is God's will to enable man to view the world on its own terms. From the viewpoint of the "Eclipse of the Secular" group the hope is that modern man might maintain and, where necessary, recover the sense of mystery and depth which lies at the heart of reality. And we discovered the persons within the "Death of the Sacred" framework to be about the task of interpreting the Christian faith from a secular perspective.

What is the *Zeitgeist* or spirit of our time? One thing is increasingly obvious concerning our present mentality; that is, it has a problem with transcendence. Kahn and Wiener have called ours a "surprise-free" world, that is, a world in which present trends continue to unfold without the intrusion of totally new and unexpected factors. More and more persons in the world are experiencing and interpreting life in a context which does not include any dimension of transcendence. The issue at stake is not easily resolvable. The secularity of our generation may indeed mean the disappearance of the sense of transcendence or possibly a radical reinterpretation as is being done by Cox, Berger, and Gilkey, for example. Cox has explored the development of a political theology and has also set forth the guidelines for understanding man as one who celebrates life. Berger has recently sought to discover the signal of transcendence in the human experiences such as play and humor. He and the European theologian Moltmann have pursued the question of transcendence into the future — hope as a sign of the "other" breaking into life. Similarly Gilkey, in his book *Naming the Whirlwind,* is found struggling with the possibility of discovering Ultimacy in secular experience. Each of these theologians has met head-on the challenge of our secular mentality. How do we speak of, or experience, God in an age which has seemingly lost touch with transcendence?

The "acids of modernity" have unmistakably had an effect upon our total life situation. The change in the climate of opinion that has come about in the Western world is the product of new understandings of history, the natural world, and human personality. The way in which these new understandings have interacted with traditional concepts must be comprehended if there is to be any reconstruction of the Christian thought which will resist the corrosive influence of the modern mind-set.

How are we to begin this process of reconstruction? Along with Gilkey we must begin with contemporary man. What is our ideal "modern man"? With Jung we would claim that "the man we call modern . . . is fully conscious of the present." [4] He is the man who is intense in his feeling for and understanding of the world situation. He is the man whose conscious awareness is maximal and whose unconsciousness concerning life is minimal. If our theological enterprise is to be beneficial, it must discover signals of transcendence in the midst of man's conscious awareness.

With the ghost of Feuerbach stirring in the background we lay claim to a theology which has anthropology as its starting point. We recognize this methodology to have come full swing in terms of the neoorthodox rejection of man, that is, its anti-anthropological stance. As Berger has pointed out in his book *A Rumor of Angels:* "If anthropology is understood here in a very broad sense, as any systematic inquiry into the constitution and condition of man, it will be clear that any kind of theology will have to include an anthropological dimension." [5] Whereas Berger proceeds to seek out what he calls "signals of transcendence" within the human experience, we shall be concerned to develop a framework within which contemporary man can both be lucid concerning his world and act on behalf of the religious tradition which is still viable.

What does it mean to reflect the needs and condition of "modern" man? What does it mean to be modern not only in the balance of our life but also in those areas of life traditionally reserved for religious faith? We know what it is to embrace life up to a point. Unless, however, we embrace modernity in terms of our faith as well, our faith will cease to have meaning and vitality for us. Such a faith has to reflect the experience of the absence of God which is a part of many people's lives. Such a faith must enable people to take the world seriously. Such a faith must be equipped with tools to help us in the recovering of the experience of transcendence. Hopefully, these demands upon our faith are the results of a correct analysis of our contemporary experience, what Gilkey calls a "hermeneutic of secular experience." [6]

This agenda has echoes of the work of Tillich and Eliade, who sought to discover the way in which religious behavior and practice became the primary driving force around which individuals ordered their lives. Richard R. Niebuhr and Thomas Luckmann have more recently been pursuing the manner in which religion functions as the "glue" in the fabric of society and as the lubrication of the historical process. We must conclude that the problem of understanding the world and taking the human condition seriously is a religious problem.

The challenge to the contemporary churchman is to get out of the box of privatized religion which is the common fare of the American church. The willingness to allow religion to deal with the private matters of life and provide sanction for the public issues is the basis and backbone of American civil religion. The billboard with the American flag and the words, "God Bless America, We Love You," is but the patriotic expression of this consensus.

The kind of privatized religion which we find in all too many of the religious institutions has been legitimately criticized by persons such as Bonhoeffer and Kierkegaard. Such religious attitudes and practices are ripe for the process of secularization. Because this emphasis upon the personal has allowed many activities or functions previously handled by the church to be assumed by secular institutions, one might conclude that modern society is becoming nonreligious.[7] If we identify religion with the institutional church, then it follows that the religious orbit varies in direct proportion to its social base; that is, its presence on street corners in cities and towns across our land is taken as an indication of our society's religious strength. This interpretation is typical of the "Sacred Against the Secular" position.

The "Sacred-Secular Paradox" position, on the other hand, with its Barthian influence has always maintained a sharp distinction between the natural religion, whose realm is the world, and the exceptional character of the Christian faith as such. This separation of sacred and secular makes the task of meaningfully integrating the various symbols and traditions which shape one's life difficult if not impossible.

The response of the "Death of the Sacred" is another option which is available whenever the credibility gap widens between traditional religious positions and contemporary life. The anti-traditionalism of radical empiricists such as Van Buren begins with radical doubt. He has undertaken to question every tradition in terms of its meaningfulness for the present.

In the face of the credibility gap which opens with every shift in the cultural scene, we have the option of proclaiming the irrelevance of religion or of accepting the demands of redefinition of religious truth. We must respond to the contemporary challenge that all institutions, ideas, and ideologies are to compete in the same marketplace. The mentality of our age challenges us to develop a world view capable of engaging people in meaningful involvement with life. We are faced with the challenge of discovering which religious traditions are capable of reflecting a new and more vigorous presence in contemporary surroundings. Our religious understanding of the world operates with a handicap which was not faced as severely by previous generations of churchmen; that is, traditional understandings of transcendence cannot be readily assumed to be meaningful. What then shall inform our world view or religious understanding?

Each and every world view has at least one dominant theme which informs its rationale. In the "Sacred Against the Secular" stance it is the inviolable nature of the faith as embodied within the evangelical church. In the "Sacred-Secular Paradox" position it is the transcendence of God and the secularity of the created order. In the "Eclipse of the Secular" schema it is the assertion that the aim of the created order and historical process can best be realized if society recognizes its dependence upon and participation in the divine ground of existence. In the "Death of the Sacred" stance it is the absence or even the death of God, the freedom of man, and the demands of secular empiricism. The religious world view which is proposed here considers the unifying theme to be religion conceived as the fundamental human response to all that shapes human existence. Within that religious understanding we shall attempt to discover whether contemporary man cannot best be understood as a political being.

Religion is the integrating motif in our world view. It is our attempt to come to grips with and interpret what is happening to us. It is our attempt to understand the cumulative "All" which shapes our lives. Religion thus becomes the umbrella experience under which man's psychological, biological, sociological, political, and economic dimensions are to be considered. From this point of view the religious man is called upon to make sense out of the multiple dimensions of existence. The religious task of each individual and each new generation is that of once more making this world its own. For one reason or another too many people are not at home in this world. The all too common experience is that of feeling secure with that which is already passing and feeling threatened by that which is becoming deeply ingrained in contemporary experience. The concerned churchman must create anew his world — bring it to birth in his experience.

This kind of creative process requires what Jung called a total consciousness of the world. This acute sensitivity to the way in which one is being shaped by one's world is a vital ingredient for the contemporary man of faith. As we discover what it means to be open to and aware of the multitude of powers and forces which shape our lives, we may be able to make sense out of what "God" means. This awareness of the forces or powers which shape our lives may lead us to conclude that the Lord of history is the Power behind the powers. To the extent that we, as people of faith, are enabled to share meaningfully in the determination of our own destinies, this understanding of our religious consciousness will become a vital part of our lives.

The contemporary urban man has an awareness of being shaped and buffeted by forces and powers, many of which are seemingly beyond his control. As men of faith our task is to make sense out of this kind of world. Beyond that we are called to enable persons to involve themselves creatively in the life process. Such an enterprise demands an image or model which provides us with the handles for coming to grips with our environment. This model we would refer to as the "religious world view" — the particular form which the religious imagination uses to appropriate and organize the world.

Out of this understanding of the faith and its relationship to the world, for example, an urban church which I served concerned itself with enabling persons to understand and live in an urban world. The urban study seminar program for high school and college age youth was designed to provide youth with the tools necessary to better understand and fully live with all the complexities and challenges of urban life. We discovered that this program not only challenged our conceptions of the way our society operates but also challenged the ability of a people of God to cope with the world. The urban study seminar was symbolic of the process which is going on continually in our lives. We are hopefully involved in the task of making the world our own — of appropriating it. This task of appropriation is a form of human creativity. We make ourselves at home in the world by creating it anew. We humanize the environment through our own or society's imagination.

The process of bringing our world to birth or of making sense out of it is never completed. The form which religious faith has peculiarly used to organize the world is the myth. Tillich and Eliade have plumbed the meaning of symbol and myth and their importance for meaningful living. Myth organizes life by dramatizing some vitality or force in people's lives and by telling a story through which this vitality is related in succeeding generations. Myths such as Genesis 1 and 2 bring the diverse field of powers and vital life-forces to birth.

The manner in which we choose our myths and stories determines the way in which we organize our world. One of the determining myths which organizes the contemporary American culture is the understanding that blacks are inferior. This story or myth has a vise-like grip on the lives of countless individuals and institutions. Another myth which is presently being challenged in our society is the role of the woman. Some women consider the interpretive story under which they have been living to be the means of their exploitation as persons and the restriction of their freedom. Both of these interpretive myths will be up for some revision in the months and years to come.

Myths allow us to relate to otherwise confusing and possibly absurd life situations. Individuals with interpretive stories capable of organizing life meaningfully for others become the spies of man's quest for the meaning of life. The myth which has been most informative of the Christian tradition has been the portrayal of Jesus of Nazareth as the Christ. The story of the carpenter from Nazareth and the particular life-style portrayed in his life and passion continues to evoke the response of the pious and even secularists such as Hamilton.

However, the portrayal of the Jesus Christ myth has not provided the same function for all persons or for every age nor has it functioned with the same clarity and intensity in every generation. But it has been the outstanding interpretive myth for the Christian church. The challenge which is posed for contemporary Christian educators is that of providing the best vehicle for maintaining the vitality of this particular tradition. There are significant differences between the portrayal of Jesus of Nazareth primarily as the Son of God and as the embodiment of a style of life. If we adopt the latter, we are then free to compare and weigh this style with others to be found in the marketplace of competing myths. Does his style provide for us the best means of responding to the world in which we live?

In our symbolic universe we discover that the role of symbols is also crucial to our gaining a grip on what is happening in our world. We can do no more than scratch the surface of the rich resources which reside in the study of symbols. An understanding of the origin and purpose of symbols provides us with needed insight into the influence and value of a particular world view. Symbols function to focus the attention and participation of individuals and social groupings. Symbols emerge as they catch up the imagination of persons involved in a significant event. They become associated with meaningful aspects or occasions in life. Water, for example, becomes more than H_2O in the symbolic rite of baptism. It symbolizes the demands and opportunities of accepting the style of life of Him who called us to deal with our death so that we might live freely.

In our Judaeo-Christian tradition, symbols such as the Exodus event continue to evoke the sense of freedom so central to the original event. Symbols may also take on the character of a theological theme such as the kingdom of God, the people of Israel, or the coming Messiah. Symbols may also be expressive of a theological affirmation such as God, the Holy Spirit, Faith, Hope, Love, or Justice.

What the man of faith can never forget is that both the hope and the hazard of symbols are grounded in history. What happens when the cultural ground or historical purpose of a particular symbol disappears? This process is illustrated particularly well in the death of the apocalyptic fever when the early church moved from being harassed to becoming the Establishment. Because of this intimate contact with culture and history, new events and the modification of cultural forms may call traditional symbolic expressions into question. Certain symbols also may receive less emphasis during one period of history than another. The concern with Christology during recent decades is a case in point. More recently the mandate has been placed upon discovering the meaningfulness of God-language.

Sometimes historical change may actually call for the eclipse, relocation, or destruction of a symbol's emphasis. We have seen this happen particularly with reference to the doctrine of God. Whether God is experienced as a wrathful warrior, a beneficial judge, a personal redeemer, an inner light, the ground of the historical process, the instigator of social revolution, absent from the historical process (or dead) depends upon the climate of the times and the perspective from which a person makes his theological observations. Thus, our understanding of God varies with our interpretation of the changing historical process. The men of faith must interpret all theological symbols, even God, in terms of the changing cultural or historical scene. The world of things, events, persons, natural resources, man-made structures, and social institutions becomes in a sense the "final filter" through which our experiences of the source of life (God) must come. Our experience of the absence of, or the possible death of, God may be due to the fact that the filter has become clogged or has ceased to function properly! Who can deny, for example, that the whole problem of pollution has revealed some short circuits in our experience of the basis of life? Our vision of that which creates and sustains life has been, in this instance, partially obscured by our facile assumptions about our ability to manipulate our environment.

This understanding of our symbols and myths as not only reflective of but also grounded in the historical process means that changes do occur in our "symbolic universe." Such change is most threatening to security-minded people. What can we really count on as being the same, yesterday, today, and forever? The authoritative nature of a theological symbol or church practice is dependent upon its ability to elicit understanding of and free involvement in the world in which we live. If a particular symbol has ceased to function in the world in which we live, it may be because the times through which we are presently passing have made it either temporarily or permanently obsolete.

The symbols and myths around which we organize our lives must include a vital understanding of not only traditional religious symbols but metaphors from nature, national life, civil organizations, cultural traditions, and the understandings of the self as well. All of these areas and more provide us with informing symbols and interpretations of the human situation which are vital if we are to cope meaningfully with life. Within the boundary of our world view must be found not only what have traditionally been referred to as theological categories but also the multitudinous expressions of all social and historical symbols. This understanding of this collection of symbols in a meaningful relationship as a "symbolic universe" comes to us from Thomas Luckmann. The problem with all too many churchmen is that their meaningful symbols travel in separate orbits around the different parts of their lives. Occasionally there occurs an event or circumstance which causes several symbols to intersect causing an "atmospheric" disturbance. Within the white American church the demonic presence of racism is such an occasion. Symbols from the Christian tradition and those which inform individuals' understandings of themselves or others have been found to be in serious conflict. The disastrous course of the nation shows the dire need for some drastic reformulation.

Churchmen who take it upon themselves to project their interpretation of life against a universal backdrop may well discover both the parochial and the authoritative nature of their symbolic life. Such an exposure of one's world view quickly shows which elements in one's mental baggage are given a new lease on life by their ability to interpret meaningfully the world in which we live. The value of our "symbolic universe" is further tested as we discover how well it becomes part of our bloodstream. For example, when the apostle Paul mentioned that he frequently did that which he *knew* he did not want to do, he was saying that although he had mentally appropriated the symbol of Jesus as the Christ, it had not yet been assimilated in his total being.

Another way of setting our sights upon the scope of our symbolic universe is to hold up what Meland calls man's historical sensibilities. Our understanding of the world is heightened as we include within our world view the meaningful experiences of previous societies. Our grounding in the meaningful traditions of the past enables us to transcend, at least in part, the urge toward obsessive relevance. The real problem for the man of faith is to hold in tension the need to be modern with the need to be historically sensitive. As each generation adds its own experience to that of the past, it adds to the storehouse of meaning and thus contributes to the progressive character of the religious world view. "The historical existence of meaning-systems is the result of universe-constructing activities of successive generations." [8]

The never-ending task of churchmen is that of enabling persons in each successive generation to take both the church and the world seriously. This process of integrating the individual into the mainstream of life is a religious "event." The success of the process is dependent upon our ability to make our own the "fabric" of meaning which holds our society together. This task has to be more than merely conforming to the meaning system of our society because there are several major flaws within that system. To allow ourselves to be uncritically shaped is to allow any lies or illusions to be mistaken for reality. This danger can be illustrated in the circumscribed nature of our nationalism and the destructive nature of our historic racism. The manner in which our culture has developed fabrications and illusions to perpetuate and condone our racism points out one particularly large flaw or crack in the symbolic universe most commonly held in our culture. To enable persons to stand back from the entanglements of our present mentality is no easy task. It requires that persons be equipped with symbolic and historical meanings which force them to take the world seriously without comfortably complying with what is.

In the dialogue of Lucy and Charlie Brown in the "Peanuts" cartoon strip we discover an essential characteristic of our task as churchmen, namely, enabling persons to live. Lucy has opened a psychiatric center and is advising Charlie Brown on his problems. His question is, "What do you do when you don't fit in? What do you do when life seems to be passing you by?" Lucy methodically lays out the world for Charlie Brown by pointing out that there are no other worlds to which one can escape. Her "priesting" word to Charlie Brown concerning this world is, "Well, live in it then!" The world in which we live may not be the one which we would have chosen, but it is, nevertheless, the world in which we are called to live. Too many of us, however, are like disillusioned Charlie Browns whose mental framework and life-styles have not enabled us to fit in and live creatively in this world.

The task of the concerned churchman is to "spy out the land." He must be able to gain entry to the world and engage it. He must be provided with a mental framework which enables him to see the way things are and hold up visions of the way things ought to be. In order to accomplish this task he must be acutely sensitive to the spirit or mentality of our age. This is an age which evaluates the world on its own terms. The church must evaluate and use the findings of secular disciplines as it establishes new directions for its traditions. To be serious about the world means also that the churchman needs to be serious about the church and its ability to inform his world understanding.

THE PROCESS OF SECULARIZATION

Although we find it almost impossible to make any final claims for the precise causes of the process of secularization, we can definitely note the effects in our Western culture. At least three particular revolutions are the focus of most discussions concerning the "process of secularization." We have already considered the changing mentality or spirit of our age. The ways in which we think are unique to our age. In the second place, the technological and industrial complex has brought changes to the mode of our lives. Finally, the resulting combination of man's thinking and habitat has brought on a transformation in his total mood.

If man is being shaped by his environment, then the anthropologists and sociologists of the future may well detect an evolution in the nature of man due to the scientific-technological revolution in which man's present life is couched. This process affects man at all levels of existence — his value system, family structure, interpersonal relationships, categories of thought, and patterns of community.[9]

A major concern in the debate regarding the process of secularization is the question of whether the Judaeo-Christian tradition has been the major cause of the cultural changes which are presently identified in the process of secularization. Have the sons of Abraham, Isaac, Jacob, the prophets, and the apostles been the major contributors to this process or not? The affirmative response to this question led persons within the "Sacred-Secular Paradox" position to celebrate the secular as the direct outgrowth of the Judaeo-Christian tradition. We therefore ask not whether but to what extent the present state of Western culture has been influenced by the biblical faith.

The changes which are a part of our Western culture are shaping individual behavior and patterns of society in ways which cannot be ignored. Technological achievements and urbanization have contributed to the pluralistic nature of society. Individuals within that society cannot escape the implications of these changes. The individual must be able to respond to the diversity of institutional forms and cultural expressions. The individual is involved in many more kinds of experiences than was the case in less complex societies. Through the wonders of the electronic age he is brought to conscious participation in facets of life of which he was previously not conscious or was unaware.

In such a situation we must sustain an enormous mental

burden. We may be repeatedly frustrated in our efforts to bring unity and coherence to our experiences. We are forced to come to grips with complexities of our civilization and culture in ways which were not heard of in the generations before mass communication and urbanization. The presence in our living rooms of televised war from Vietnam, radical confrontations between students or minority groups and the police, and the overwhelming effects of space exploration have literally "blown our minds." The secular man is the one who has been able to maintain a lucid awareness of what is happening to him and his world.

Marty has argued that in the American scene ". . . secularization did *not* mean the disappearance of religion so much as its relocation." [10] If this is the case, then some fundamental questions need to be raised concerning the status of contemporary religiosity. In spite of the fact that our society is dominated by the urban milieu our religiosity is so frequently anti-urban. The anti-urban mythology which is so deeply rooted in much of American culture religion is disastrously destructive of efforts to take the present world situation seriously. The illusory phrase, "God made the country, man made the city," is no longer viable. Such a view, which romanticizes the natural world and the countryside, yet holds many reservations and suspicions about man-made cities, inhibits the necessary reformulation of traditional categories of thought. Such illusions are to be broken by recognizing that the Word is to be found in the midst of the concrete and steel as well as in the midst of the lakes and rills and templed hills or it will not be found at all. The relocation of religion of which Marty speaks is the continued accent upon the private nature of religiosity rather than its public demands.

The contemporary churchman who rests content with a privatized religion will find himself bewildered when trying to cope with the chaotic events and expressions of the contemporary culture. The events of the last decade have led us repeatedly to ask, "What the hell is happening in our society?" This is basically a religious question. Our religious world view should be equipped to deal with such a fundamental question. To the extent that either we fail to grasp or we misinterpret the contemporary scene, our thought-patterns or styles of living may be threatened by change or secularization.

The danger which is fundamental to contemporary American religiosity is that it has become comfortable with disparity. That is, it has not maintained a prophetic stance toward the illusions of our society such as racism, a sentimental nationalism, and national priorities which are out of joint. A religious stance which is comfortable with the demonic waste of national resources in war and urban decay while resting content with a faith which addresses only individual and personal problems is living a most schizophrenic existence. This emphasis upon the individual characterizes the "Sacred Against the Secular" stance in which the blame for such disparity between faith and life is placed upon individuals who must be "converted" before things will be made right.

Another option for dealing with the disparity between one's religious world view and the condition of contemporary life is to dispose of the world view in its entirety and to formulate an explicitly secular value system *de novo*. One sees in the programmatic efforts of the "Death of the Sacred" stance such an attempt. This alienation from or apathy toward the church and its traditions is increasingly evident in the urban setting where the church is so threatened with extinction. The increasing attitude is one of "I'm from Missouri, show me!" "Just try to persuade me that the church and its traditions mean anything."

Somewhere between the evangelical and the secularist positions there are a number of options open to those churchmen who wish to wrestle with the disparity between the Christian world view and the contemporary life situation. If we are to be faithful to the original function of the religious tradition, which is to supply the individual with an interpretive model for meaningfully coming to grips with diverse realms of life, then our world view must be continually refined and redefined so that we might enable persons to integrate their lives.

Such reinterpretation and reformulation of our theological world view in order to make sense out of the contemporary scene is not an easy task. How do we avoid reflecting the culture in which we live, after the pattern of American culture religion so prevalent in the churches? Only a world view which meaningfully addresses the world is worthy of becoming an "official model." Such a world view will be capable of integrating and legitimating the numerous involvements and styles of conduct called for in the routines as well as the crises of existence. Through the process of secularization many aspects of the traditional world view have not only been called into question by the changing times, but alternative modes of interpreting life have replaced tradition.

The credibility gap between modern life and tradition comes about, in part, because the theological custodians have failed in their educational task to bring the laymen into twentieth-century channels of faith. The instant popularity of Bishop Robinson's book *Honest to God* sharply illustrated the fact that the thought life of the seminaries had failed miserably to filter down to the local church level. When Robinson's book appeared, theologians merely yawned. They felt that his thought was merely "Tillich made popular and understandable." But his readable book became the vehicle by which many laymen were brought to consider for the first time the crises of faith in the contemporary church.

Another reason for the continual problem of secularization involves what we shall refer to as the "built-in obsolescence" of some religious symbols. Some traditions or symbols outlive their usefulness and attempt to claim a hearing even though they may be irrelevant. One example comes from the experience of the early church. The expectation of the return of Jesus following his death became a problem for the church. Whenever the social climate was right, the eschatological fervor of Christ's return caught on. Since he did not return as expected, church plans had to be adjusted accordingly. Some adherents of the church took that opportunity to cast serious doubt upon the total truth of Christian doctrine. Others, following the lead of the apostle Paul, chose the wiser course of recognizing that mistakes have been made in the interpretation of even something as cherished as the meaning of the life of Jesus of Nazareth.

With varying degrees of success the church has functioned throughout history as the preserver and interpreter of the Judaeo-Christian tradition. Because the church as an institution embodies both that which is relevant and that which is obsolete within that tradition, it is constantly threatened by the process of secularization. The more complex society becomes, the more difficulty the church will have in maintaining the religious tradition in its most vital form. Those who have claimed that the church is obsolete are really harbingers of an eschatological phenomenon. "And I saw no temple in the city, for its temple is the Lord God the Almighty and the Lamb" (Revelation 21:22). The realization of the temple-less city is not to be found in any of the secular cities of this generation, but must await the new age.

The function of the church is to embody and validate not only those traditions which are peculiar to her Judaeo-Christian tradition but also the multitude of other historical symbols which are essential for development of a meaningful relationship with the world. As tensions develop between these religious and historical traditions and symbols, the task of the churchman is to once more integrate the world view. As channels of openness to the contemporary culture are developed, institutional stagnation is combated. As Luckman relates:

> A serious problem of institutional specialization of religion consists, therefore, in the fact that the "official" model of religion changes at a slower rate than the "objective" social conditions that codetermine the predominant individual systems of "ultimate" significance.[11]

In that compact statement we are given the challenge to the church posed by the historical process. Individual churchmen must be enabled to take with integrity both the world and the church seriously without compromising either. If the forces with which we contend in life shape us in ways which create tensions within our religious world view, then some remodeling of our world view is needed.

We all recognize that the times are changing. What is important is whether or not we are able to restructure our total world view so that we are enabled to embrace change. We feel more secure when things remain "nailed down." Not until a Freud, a Copernicus, a Darwin, or a James Forman threatens our basic assumptions will we consider change.

As the seventies opened, two severe challenges pressed upon our religious consciousness, one institutional and the other theological in nature. The institutional question has been most sharply illustrated by the barrage leveled at the church by James Forman and the Black Manifesto. The theological question is the God-question about the possibility of the experience of transcendence. On the one hand the contemporary churchman is unsure of the experience of transcendence, while, on the other hand, he is accused of being a part of an institution whose ethics are questionable. If we are to move meaningfully in the decade of the seventies, we must deal with these two thorny issues. How do we deal meaningfully with the ever-present problem of transcendence, and how does the church relate to the turmoil of the times?

Recent books by Berger and Gilkey have made it extremely clear that the question of transcendence is crucial for us. As Berger remarks, "We are, whether we like it or not, in a situation in which transcendence has been reduced to a rumor." [12] Each of us keeps the rumor alive in his own way. The way in which we handle the problem of transcendence or the way in which we keep the rumor alive is usually a good indication of the agenda which we are providing for the church as an institution as well.

In the last unit of this chapter we will be exploring together one way of dealing with the problem of transcendence and the future of the church. Recognizing that we have attempted to bring our world together and dispel the dichotomy between the sacred and the secular, our agenda becomes more clearly defined. Beyond that we accepted the "worldly" nature of the world and are thus serious about developing a "theology of the world." Such a theology will hopefully discover the sacred through the secular realm.

In order to get at the heart of the issue most quickly we will address the theological problem of our religious world view in terms of the most secular thing that we can think of — politics. If there is anything which the average person is confused by, hostile toward, made nervous in the presence of, or angered by reference to; it is politics! However, the embrace of the political arena of life will provide us with some basic clues toward understanding man, the human situation, and the most pressing theological dilemma — the existence of God.

We will hopefully find in the following discussion that the political nature of life is the glue which not only holds man meaningfully within the social fabric but which also provides signals of the "depths" of life as well.

RELIGION AND CHRISTIANITY

> "Man is a political animal!"
> Aristotle

From the previous discussion one can readily see that the need for maintaining the religious tradition and related institutions has not been minimized. The man of faith needs a religious system of belief and an institution which supports his faith style in the public arena. If traditions and symbols are to be sustained over the span of successive generations, then they must be institutionalized. Thomas Luckmann points out that a particular world view:

> . . . originates in human activities that are at least partly institutionalized. It is transmitted over the generations in processes that are, again, at least partly dependent on institutions. Conversely, performances and institutions depend on the continuous internalization of a world view.[13]

Luckmann's depiction is similar to what Tillich has in mind as he cites the importance of the "vocational consciousness" of a history-bearing group. "History runs in a horizontal direction, and the groups which give it this direction are determined by an aim toward which they strive and a destiny they try to fulfill."[14] The challenge for the man of faith is to sort out what is the appropriate "aim" of the tradition which he feels called to sustain and what are the methods necessary to fulfill the destiny of the common humanity which he shares.

We must recognize that institutions may also perpetuate the stifling of the human spirit. The privatizing of religious practice was interpreted by Kierkegaard and Bonhoeffer as demonic in their respective generations. We must recognize here that the same institution may indeed maintain the demonic nature and strength of racism as well as provide us with glimpses of what participatory democracy can be like.

The religious challenge for the contemporary man of faith is to discover how to strengthen those aspects of the institutional church which have maintained a vital function in the humanizing process while attempting to renew those parts of the institution which have grown stagnant with time. In recent years we have seen many experiments within and outside of the church with forms of celebration and mission which are worthy of being maintained and strengthened. We must be careful not to lose these "happenings" in the contemporary mania for the new and different. In the tradition of Max Weber these "happenings" need to be "routinized." Happenings have a continued effect only as they are institutionalized. The church as an institution needs to be measured by the visions of the future and the kinds of traditions which are necessary for addressing that future.

The effectiveness of the church and adherents of the faith will greatly depend upon the ability of their world view to provide individuals with a sufficient grasp of the historical process. Such a world view will provide individuals with models, interpretive schemes or "recipes" for conduct, to meet the demands and diversities of a given social setting. Within the world view itself all symbols of meaning cannot claim the same priority; that is, they will be ranked by what Luckmann refers to as an "inner hierarchy of significance." At the lowest level we respond out of habit to concrete objects and routine events. At the opposite end of the continuum we find those symbols of meaning which are least accessible and the most problematical. For example, tying our shoes does not pose too much of a problem for us, but the question of our vocation or the problem of the renewal of our core cities may cause severe anxiety. A view of the world must embody this total spectrum and enable churchmen to relate meaningfully to it.

Within this hierarchy individuals and institutions have held up various aspects of belief and practice as most essential and important. We have pointed out from time to time that the contemporary American church is most characterized by its accent upon private, personal problems. This one-sided emphasis of the faith fails to provide us with the means for understanding or relating to man as a social being or public decision-maker. But from the public arena comes the primary assault of secularization. In the public arena our lives are being decisively shaped and our destinies are being de-

termined. The challenge for the church today is the development of a "public" theology.

By public is meant a theology and religious belief system
which enables persons to live out their lives in the public
arena. If the church and the man of faith are not able to
compete in that public arena, the importance of the church and
religious faith for the future of our communities and society
is going to be severely limited. For the most part the church
has not yet been very effective in developing such a public
strategy.

To be "public," as opposed to or in addition to being
"private" in our faith, is, in the language of the evangelist, to
be concerned with our corporate souls as well as our individual or private lives. A public theology may also be termed
a "political theology"! This kind of theological alternative was
brought to our attention by Harvey Cox and others but has
most recently been developed more fully by J. B. Metz.
Political theology — does it make any sense? Is it just another
gimmick to avoid the kind of hard realism which faces theologians and churchmen today? Is it just a means to provide
justification for the political activism which some contemporary
clergy and laymen find exciting?

What does it mean to project the possibility of a political
theology? First of all, we are called to take most seriously the
nature of our contemporary mental attitude and framework
provided for us by science, technology, and urbanization. To
develop a political theology is to recognize man's growing
power to alter his destiny and that of all living beings, as well
as being aware of the increasing interdependence of men
with each other, with nature, and with the machines they
create. A political theology recognizes that contemporary man
has the power to direct the course of history toward goals of
his own choosing. He has taken up the creative task. If politics
has to do with the ordering of the community of man for the
sake of the good life, then a political theology would be about
the task of developing a symbolic framework and style of
life capable of shaping a vision of the good life as well as
realizing it.

The agenda before us calls us to take seriously the political
nature and possibilities of our fellowman. We are beset from

all sides by political issues — cries for revolution, clamor for a fairer distribution of wealth and power, and demands for a more participatory democracy. The current ferment points up the fact that we are going through a period of transition. Our society and our communities are changing. Whether the church and the traditions of faith out of which we live are able to be effective change agents is highly dependent upon whether a political theology and style is developed. The American situation provides the church with the gift of human need shaped by the unspeakable mess of the domestic and international situation. The theological tradition and style which best addresses this contemporary condition may well enable the church to take the liberating "leap" from ambiguity to commitment.

A threatening factor in developing a political theology is the fragile nature of relevance. The memories of the secular city celebrations which have become nightmares are all too fresh in our minds. Recognizing that our cultural life does not allow for much permanency does not minimize the need for developing the decision-making processes and viable communities through direct political reflection and action.

One of the primary ways of discovering what political theology or a political style is like is to define what it is not. The kind of religious style which is the opposite of the politically sensitive religious style is privatized religion. Religiosity in America has for too long been defined in terms of the private concerns of persons rather than the public or political dimensions of life. Political theology is a critical correction of the extreme privatizing tendency of this contemporary religiosity. This privatized religious style is found to be most prevalent within the evangelical tradition of the "Sacred Against the Secular" stance. The practice of faith is therein reduced to a timeless decision of the person. This kind of individualized faith has always been very compatible with the American Dream. The heroes of the past and present are those persons who conquered the wilderness, gained incredible wealth, or overcame personal problems by their own individual resources.

The most demonic expression of this privatizing of the faith within American culture religion is racism in our society.

The failure to understand the institutional nature of life and the history of oppression which our society has leveled against blacks allows whites to hide their racism behind this rather substantial blind spot. The persons who are content to allow the faith to keep guard over the personal future without recognizing the social nature of their lives are definitely akin to and possibly partially responsible for the present condition of our divided society.

Allowing the faith to remain private is a "security blanket" which our society can ill afford. *"The deprivatizing of theology is the primary critical task of political theology."* [15] But enabling people of God to reclaim the public arena in behalf of the prophetic nature of faith is not an easy task. Those churchmen who initiated the process of making public their theology in the civil rights movement, war protest, draft resistance, or any number of other more local political issues have recognized quite well that most people just do not want to see the public arena as their responsibility. They consider public expressions of faith beyond giving the invocation at the local Lions Club to be just plain meddling! Involvement with critical life issues is politics, and politics is still basically a dirty word in church circles. The church is held by most people to be above politics. She is thought to be able to accomplish her mission without using power because she is a truly "spiritual" community.

One of the things which happens to individual churches or denominational bodies when members begin to involve themselves politically is that the entire body is frequently politicized. We have seen the emergence of a number of political caucuses within denominational bodies, some as the initiators of change and others in reaction to the political tactics employed by other caucuses. Persons and churches are being politicized in reaction to the kinds of political issues being considered in church assemblies. Denominational budgets are feeling the pressure put on them by churches opposed to certain controversial ministries involved with housing, community organization work, draft counseling, or courses directed at white racism.

The kind of polarizing politics which has been most commonly experienced within the church has dealt with the role of the clergy as the custodians of tradition within the church and even the society. This contest of politics between clerics and laity and between churches of differing theological persuasions is only the beginning of the politicizing of the man of faith. The real task of making our faith style political deals with the world around us and not primarily with disagreements between churches and churchmen who share differing faith styles. But at least the struggle that does exist points up the increasing awareness that the faith when expressed has political consequences. Enabling persons to develop a political style out of their faith understanding is the task of the minister and theologian.

The crux of political theology is the development of a theological understanding which places the human individual within the context of a human society. Saul Alinsky, that theological non-theologian, pointed out several decades ago the kind of action which is needed to humanize communities. He saw clearly and perceptively the powerlessness of mere words and the personally rewarding nature of justice-oriented actions. In his book *Reveille for Radicals,* he provides some guidelines for doing and acting out a political theology. Alinsky's use of the word "radical" is far different from the inflammatory tactics of contemporary revolutionaries although many of the issues are the same. He speaks of the radical as the one who has great sensitivity toward human rights. In setting the radical over against the liberal, Alinsky provides us with some instructive insights into a basic problem in the life of the church — how are people enabled to go beyond merely thinking right to that critically important level of acting out of their faith understanding? As Alinsky puts it, "Liberals like people with their heads, radicals like people with both their heads and their *hearts.*"[16]

The number of churchmen who are radical in the sense in which Alinsky uses the term is much too few. Something which needs to be learned from some of Alinsky's confrontation tactics as well as from the politicizing efforts of certain radical youth is that people can be fundamentally changed. That is, persons can be enabled not only to see and articulate clearly an understanding of the human situation in which they find themselves but that they can be brought to act out of that understanding as well. The Democratic National Convention which was held in Chicago in August of 1968 provided us with a most clear example of this. Many people found it relatively easy to recognize the undemocratic nature of political processes within the society and of particular decisions related to convention week. But not until some of them got caught in the middle of, or were firsthand witnesses to, some of the insanities of those political decisions were they truly convinced, or "radicalized"!

Enabling persons not only to be lucid about the human and political conditions in which their lives are cast but also to internalize that understanding as part of their life-style is a worthy calling of political theology. This "convincing" process is seemingly best accomplished "on location." That is, individuals are best enabled to act out of their faith understanding in its public dimensions when they have been exposed to firsthand experiences of how that faith is tied into life.

The current tragedy of such a sensitive political awareness and related style of action is that "common sense has become radical," as Harrington puts it in his book *Toward a Democratic Left*.[17] Those in our midst who have gained a fresh sense of human worth as over against property values, who have sensed the need for "politicizing" as opposed to "economizing," have been branded as radicals and worse. If, however, our communities and nation as a whole are effectively to defuse the violence and destructiveness of segments of our youth and minority groups, we must enable increasing numbers of people within our society to organize themselves politically and share in the common destiny.

If we are to talk about having faith in life, in the structures and processes which shape our existence, we must say that the America of the seventies displays an increasing lack of faith at several critical levels of society. To the extent that the political process has been removed from the people, to the extent that people do not share in the control over their own lives, they have a faith problem. Many persons are becoming increasingly aware that the kinds of things which are accepted as normal in our society are wrong and that many individuals are seemingly helpless to do anything about it. In the words of Tillich their sense of "freedom and destiny" is out of joint.

For Tillich the freedom-destiny polarity is an ontological category. If a person participates in life to the extent that he has the freedom of deliberation, decision, and responsible action and recognizes that his destiny is emerging out of his free choice, then that person is experiencing one of the depths of life. Another way of putting it might be to say that transcendence is experienced in the power to decide the act. He who is either not free or whose destiny does not call forth his full humanity is cut off from experiencing transcendence to one degree or another. This kind of freedom is not an abstraction, but it is like the political and social emancipation of ancient Israel from the taskmasters of Egypt. The promise or destiny of God's people was not empty but was given in terms of the land which God showed his people.

The New Left does not speak of participating in the polarity of freedom and destiny but does refer to "participatory democracy." Theologically, these two concepts may be blood brothers! A sense of transcendence or the experience of depth may be recovered by those who come to celebrate the possibilities of entering into and meaningfully shaping those processes which determine their future destinies. We have heard much of late in theological circles of the "theology of hope." The real question which must be asked of those who advocate a hope-filled theology is whether it is grounded in political realism. If it is not, it can be as disillusioning as a "Great Society" unrealized.

To speak of a theology of hope having political realism or to refer to the public nature of the faith can still leave us with a political theology which has not moved beyond the academic or reflective level. Only as we "take to the streets" can our theology receive its most fundamental political test. If those streets are in Chicago, then everything that one does is *political!* In this city to touch its pulse is to sense the political nature of life. Whether one is pleading in the courts, seeking building code enforcement, receiving welfare, living in an urban renewal area, seeking to get out of a traffic violation, wanting more strict enforcement of pollution regulations, or trying to open a day care center; his life is shaped by the political nature of things.

A real problem for the practicing theologian or churchman

is that he is most likely still inflicted with that theological mononucleosis known as the "gentle-Jesus-meek-and-mild" disease. We have been told that the "meek shall inherit the earth" while repeatedly witnessing political eunuchs being ground down by the processes of society. There is the famous aphorism that comes from Lord Acton, the British historian, which we most likely have heard from time to time: "Power tends to corrupt. Absolute power corrupts absolutely." If we read this affirmation to say that power is synonymous with corruption we then would accept as an ideal condition of human nature that of powerlessness — impotence.

The apostle Paul was not one who was so obsessed with meekness. He says in his second letter to Timothy, "For God did not give us a spirit of timidity but a spirit of power and love and self-control" (2 Timothy 1:7). If we can avoid spiritualizing this bit of advice, we are provided with a political mandate to provide individuals with enough power for self-determination and a sense of destiny.

The biblical faith sees man as an historical and social creature whose aim is to be confident in the ultimately reliable power. This faith defines and fulfills the destiny of man as an individual and of man in community. In a fundamental fashion this faith is expressed in the Exodus experience. God is a dynamic power that has liberated man from slavery. He has brought a people out of Egypt and has guided them across the Red Sea and the wilderness. This power of God's makes a covenant of faithfulness with the people.

The most reliable power in the Old Testament witness is the divine community-forming power. This skill of organizing and reconciling people in community is also one of the vital functions of the early New Testament churches. The calling of the contemporary churchman is to extend the field of participation in power to the powerless. Thus persons may be enabled to become fully conscious of and actively participate in the decision-making processes of society. However, numerous individuals and groups of people are not in a position to participate in the shaping of that which determines their lives even though they have a conscious desire to do so. Such individuals are the anonymous, readily replaceable men of the labor market, the blacks or other minorities upon whom impotence has been effectively imposed, and others subject to a combination of factors which cause them to become alienated from the mainstream of life.

Thus we are called to redefine not only the processes of power but also the quality of purpose of such participation. We might say that what is needed is "imaginative politics," or a participatory democracy which has been sufficiently infused with humanizing goals. Blessed are the powerful who acknowledge that their power is a gift that imposes ever new responsibilities and offers ever new, though costly, joys. To recognize the need for a political theology is to be aware that the structure of society ultimately either enables man to be human or perpetuates dehumanization. The role of the church is to strengthen the participation of individuals in the decision-making processes which determine their destinies as well as to call into question those powers and principalities which are destroying genuine humanness.

The theological-political task in terms of the powerless is to enable them to discover the meaning of power and to come to share in it. Power! Power is the capacity to participate in the life-shaping process. The graffiti which we need to write on the sides of the buildings in our communities is "Love Thy Neighbor, but Organize Him!" Socialize the power relationship. Free the political eunuchs to become fully human. Anyone who has witnessed a powerless person taste genuine power for the first time recognizes that such an event is an experience of transcendence or a signal thereof.

The question which we must ask of our theology is whether it enables us or hinders us in terms of political involvement. If it is the former, then we are well on our way toward developing a political theology. Such a theology means more than encouraging our congregations to vote on election day. It means entering into the process of selection of and campaigning for political candidates who most closely embody participatory democracy. When the regular political party structure falters, then the development of a strong independent political organization may be able to bring politics to the people. Churchmen and religious leaders who have become directly involved in political campaigns have shared a real koinonia and ecumenism.

If, however, the democratic process is not capable of sharing sufficient power and responsibility with certain communities, if the political arteries have hardened, it may be necessary to develop alternative political structures capable of dealing effectively with the structures of power. The most notable example of this alternate structure is to be found in the community organization pattern developed by Saul Alinsky and the Industrial Areas Foundation.

The call for the development of a political theology can mean the understanding of politics as a Christian vocation. Increasing numbers of theologically trained persons are "going political" either through direct involvement in political processes or else through related thrusts such as community organization work. Individuals with a theological or religious consciousness who have become involved in either of these ways have frequently concluded that they find more meaning in the political arena than in traditional church life. This discovery might well be added to the "signals of transcendence" which Berger has listed.

Politics as a vocation means the development of a political life-style informed by one's faith. There is an increasing need for persons to take up the vocation of influencing the distribution and effective use of power in our communities. If one is in the urban core, the task is that of enabling persons to gain control over their own destinies. If one is in the affluent regions of our society, the task is to call for the sharing of and wise use of political power.

Involvement with precinct politics on Chicago's North Side has brought to me not only an increasing awareness of how the "machine" in Chicago operates, but also many insights about what needs to be done in order that people might be freed to engage meaningfully in the political process. Leaving politics to the politicians has a deadening effect upon the lives of persons and communities. There is something about "ringing doorbells" in a hotly contested political campaign which pumps energy into one's theological system. There is something about educating persons to the political issues which tests the basis of many of one's theological tenets as well as one's understanding of how the society works. The theological test may come in the form of one's own struggle to develop a political theology. If it doesn't come at that point, it will most definitely come from irate laymen who refuse to allow clergy or laymen to become involved in politics on behalf of the church. But such a test is just what the serious churchman needs. He needs to be aware of whether his theological world view is capable of taking the world seriously in this fashion.

The theological image which has poured vitality into my understanding political theology is that of Nathan's visit to King David. There is something so refreshingly candid about that confrontation which addresses a word to those who are involved in politically doing theology. While we may not be able to "catch the conscience of the king" in just that manner, the biblical drama drives home to us the fact that there was a time in the history of our faith when politics was not reserved to the professional politicians and religion was not content with "doing its own thing"! That unified image of the kingdom of God needs to inform our theology. With Nathan we are called to address the political realities through word and confrontation. We must recognize the responsibility which is ours to call the political process to serve the people.

Our communities and society have reached levels of disrepair which call for more than mere "meddling in politics"! The times call for us to pick up our theological baggage and run the gauntlet of political realism. There is a close connection between breaking persons open to take the church seriously and enabling them to take the world seriously. Models for accomplishing this task are to be found in those political movements which are "radicalizing" people. Becoming lucid about the world and the way things operate and relating that understanding to the demands of faith can no longer be accomplished within the seclusion of the sanctuary. Political theology calls us to take to the streets. This style of involvement was dramatized for us in civil rights activity, radicalized in campus confrontations, televised in the Democratic Convention in Chicago in 1968, and demonstrated in court proceedings regarding radical students and the conspiracy laws.

The effective test of one's theological world view is whether one can make sense out of our current situation and beyond that propose and work for creative solutions to contemporary problems. The test of one's theology is whether one is able to enter meaningfully into the dynamics of this politicizing process. The test of the church in the seventies will most surely include its ability to relate to communities and persons experiencing powerlessness. The test of the man of faith will involve his ability to make sense out of the alternatives to power in the public arena and to align himself with those agents of power which most directly reflect the biblical call to justice and righteousness.

We began this chapter with the God-question and will end it at that point. The contemporary theologian may decide whether he wants to begin his faith system with politics or metaphysics. If we choose to begin with the former, we cannot, however, avoid the metaphysical question. The political approach just gives us the context for dealing meaningfully with the metaphysical or God-question.

If we are correct in holding up political theology as one meaningful way of getting beyond the current theological impasse, then we may find some clarity as far as our understanding of God is concerned. Without pretending that the following remarks are in any way exhaustive, they will provide some guidelines for further developing a political theology.

If our analysis of political participation has been correct, then it does provide us with one of the signals of transcendence available to contemporary man. Such discovery of transcendence through political participation also says something about the God whom we serve. It says that he is a political God who is somehow the power behind the political powers. If we can become more fully aware of that which shapes our lives in the public arena, we might have clues to understanding what it means to discern those powers as extensions of The Power. If participatory democracy provides us with the best political model for enabling individuals and communities to become fully human, then our understanding of God must also be democratized!

CONCLUDING REMARKS

The fundamental nature of the God-question has by no means been resolved in this discussion. We have held up some of the crucial reasons why the existence of God and the nature of faith is being peculiarly challenged in our day. We have tried to pursue some of the alternatives to the contemporary theological situation. The suggestiveness of political theology may provide us with some of the ingredients for a thriving theological future.

So we stand with people of God in the decade called the seventies. We recognize that trying to be faithful to the tradition and serious about the world may strain our patience. So we weep with those who mourn the passing of previous familiar expressions of faith and rejoice with those who embrace the challenges of the new day.

The condition of our times and the state of the church say something about the future of theology for the man of faith. We have attempted to hold up "theological politics" as a live option for the contemporary churchman. This includes a faith stance which is not only serious about the faith tradition but which is also serious about the world situation. This is a theological option which can clarify the contradictions of our time through critical analysis of the faith stance.

Political theology calls for men of faith who are not only agents or enablers of change but who are also equipped to celebrate change. We have set our discussion of political theology within the larger purview of a religious world view. There we were careful to preserve the symbolic or imaginal nature of man and the ingredients of faith. It might be said that the man of faith is called to possess or respond to imaginal politics. That is, his life must not only be set against the realism of the political arena but he must also be equipped to hold up the images of a just and humane society which call forth creative response.

Our benediction to the church is to "be political but celebrate life as well." In the areas of politics and celebration at least one young churchman has found the vitality of the ministry to be expressed. Political involvement has tested the faithfulness of the church and celebration has illuminated the lifelessness of so many aspects of our communities and individual lives. Imaginal politics has brought one community of faith to wrestle with the realities of the political arena but also to experience how the celebration of worship has been informed by that involvement.

What is man? Man is both a political animal and a celebrator. In political involvement the mandate of faith is carried out. In celebration the images of faith are spun out and clarified. It is hoped that this projection of the possibilities of a political theology have set the stage for man to fulfill his imaginal and political capacities in a meaningful fashion. May our encounter with imaginal or theological politics enable us to provide some possible new directions for the contemporary churchman.

Peace and Courage!

Chart of Sacred-Secular Relationships

CHART OF SACRED-SECULAR RELATIONSHIPS

	The Secular	Secularity	The Process of Secularization	Religion and Christianity
The Sacred Against the Secular	The secular world is the realm of forces and ideas which threaten the life of faith as preserved in the church. God works through the church's faithful.	The secular mentality which limits itself to this-worldly criteria is a threat to the Christian orientation toward transcendence.	The process of secularization threatens the future of the church because it involves the withdrawal of areas of life and activity from the control of organized religious bodies—the church.	Religion as defined by culture has no place in the life of faith as proclaimed by the church.
The Sacred-Secular Paradox	Since God is utterly transcendent, there are no secular absolutes. The world has been liberated from all religious absolutes.	It is to be celebrated that modern man is no longer bound by religious absolutes. The modern mind is shaped by the total culture; its orientation is functional.	The process of secularization is the providence of God at work in the world. Man is thus demanded to reorient himself to a world which no longer is primarily religious.	Christianity must be religionless if the world is to remain truly secular. Religion is here defined as need-fulfilling individualism or provision for a "God of the gaps."
The Eclipse of the Secular	All of life is responsible to the sacred order. The secular includes those	The mentality which is not responsive to the sacred is not capable of	The eclipse of religious expressions and traditional symbols is a	Religion is the substance of culture. The maintenance of religious

	maverick areas which have been withdrawn from religious influence or control.	understanding the depth and complexity of life.	threat to man's nature and existence. The sacred perspective must be recovered in full.	sensitivities is central to the appropriation of life in depth.
The Death of the Sacred	Everything is secular since God is meaningless for contemporary man.	Because the world is self-explanatory, the modern mind can no longer conceive of God. All traditional religious symbolism must be interpreted in a secular fashion.	The process of secularization has not only eroded traditional religious symbols but has eclipsed the reality of God as well.	The attempt to make Christianity viable for secular man may mean the development of a secular "religious" cult.
The Sacred Through the Secular	The secular is not a realm apart from the sacred. It stands for our world. Traditional religious institutions and symbols are one dimension of the various expressions of our culture. Our experience is of God's absence]	The mentality of our age is primarily shaped by the cultural symbols expressive of our technological society. This mentality needs to be open to the historical as well as the contemporary experience of religious and cultural symbols.	Ways of thought and modes of existence are being altered. There is, however, dialogue between traditional religious symbols and the cultural scene. One's religious stance forms the basis for one's appropriation of the world.	Religion is man's response to that which shapes him ultimately. Institutional religion needs to be open to the imaginal and symbolic nature of life and grounded in a political style which enables the oppressed and the powerless to achieve human dignity and worth.

Notes

CHAPTER 1 — STRANGERS IN A STRANGE LAND

[1] Larry Shiner, "Toward a Theology of Secularization," *The Journal of Religion,* vol. 45 (October, 1965), p. 279.

CHAPTER 2 — THE SACRED AGAINST THE SECULAR

[1] John Charles Cooper, *Radical Christianity and Its Sources* (Philadelphia: The Westminster Press, 1968), p. 45.

[2] Philip Arthur Micklem, *The Secular and Sacred* (London: Hodder and Stoughton, Limited, 1948), p. 39.

[3] Egbert De Vries, ed., *Man in Community: Christian Concern for the Human in Changing Society* (New York: Association Press, 1966), p. 323.

[4] Harry Blamires, *The Christian Mind* (New York: The Seabury Press, 1963), p. 16.

[5] Reinhold Niebuhr, "The King's Chapel and the King's Court," *Christianity and Crisis* (August 4, 1969), p. 212.

[6] Blamires, *op. cit.,* p. 3.

[7] Martin Marty, *The Modern Schism: Three Paths to the Secular* (New York: Harper & Row, Publishers, 1969), p. 122.

[8] *Ibid.,* p. 123.

[9] Lesslie Newbigin, *Honest Religion for Secular Man* (Philadelphia: The Westminster Press, 1966), p. 49.

[10] Jacques Ellul, *The Technological Society*, trans. John Wilkinson (New York: Alfred A. Knopf, Inc., 1964), p. 84.

[11] *Ibid.*, p. 42.

[12] From the University of Minnesota's *Minnesota Daily* (February 14, 1967), as quoted in "Evangelical Springtime," *The Christian Century* (1967), p. 575.

[13] Martin Marty, *et al.*, *What Do We Believe?* (Des Moines: Meredith Press, 1968), p. 28.

[14] Soren Kierkegaard, *Kierkegaard's Attack upon "Christendom,"* trans. Walter Lowrie (Boston: Beacon Press, 1944), pp. 34-35.

[15] Marty, *The Modern Schism*, pp. 98-100.

[16] *Ibid.*, p. 132.

[17] Martin Marty, *The Search for a Usable Future* (New York: Harper & Row, Publishers, 1969), p. 68.

CHAPTER 3 — THE SACRED-SECULAR PARADOX

[1] Bernard Meland, *The Secularization of Modern Cultures* (New York: Oxford University Press, 1966), p. 145.

[2] Harvey Cox, *The Secular City* (New York: The Macmillan Company, 1965), p. 31.

[3] Eric Hoffer, *The Temper of Our Time* (New York: Harper & Row, Publishers, 1967), p. 20, as quoted in Martin Marty, *The Modern Schism: Three Paths to the Secular* (New York: Harper & Row, Publishers, 1969), p. 9.

[4] Colin Williams, *Faith in a Secular Age* (New York: Harper & Row, Publishers, 1966), p. 25.

[5] Cornelius Van Peursen, "Men and Reality — The History of Human Thought," *The Student World* (Supplement No. 1, 1963), pp. 13-19.

[6] Cox, *op. cit.*, p. 60.

[7] *Ibid.*, pp. 80-81.

[8] Martin Marty, *et al.*, *What Do We Believe?* (Des Moines: Meredith Press, 1968), p. 32.

[9] *Ibid.*

[10] C. G. Jung, *Modern Man in Search of a Soul*, trans. W. S. Dell and Cary F. Baynes (New York: Harcourt, Brace and World, Inc., 1939), pp. 226-227.

[11] Carl Friedrich Von Weizsäcker, *The Relevance of Science: Creation and Cosmogony* (London: Collins, 1964), p. 162.

[12] Arend Th. Van Leeuwen, *Christianity in World History: The Meeting of the Faiths of East and West*, trans. H. H. Hoskins (London: Edinburgh House Press, 1964), p. 331.

[13] Cox, *op. cit.*, p. 17.

[14] Von Weizäcker, *op. cit.*, p. 50.

[15] *Ibid.*, p. 107.

[16] Larry Shiner, *The Secularization of History: An Introduction to the Theology of Friedrich Gogarten* (Nashville: Abingdon Press, 1966), p. 20.

[17] *Ibid.*, pp. 26-30.

[18] *Ibid.*, p. 35.

[19] For those interested in pursuing this matter further, a helpful resource is found in an article by James L. Adams, "The Law of Nature in Greco-Roman Thought," *The Journal of Religion*, vol. 25 (April, 1945), pp. 97-118.

[20] Shiner, *op. cit.*, p. 1.

[21] Larry Shiner, "Toward a Theology of Secularization," *The Journal of Religion*, vol. 45 (October, 1965), p. 285.

[22] Martin Jarrett-Kerr, "The Secular: Substitute, Challenge, or Heir Apparent?" *Religion in Life*, vol. 35 (Winter, 1965-1966), p. 27.

[23] Cox, *op. cit.*, p. 1.

[24] Martin Marty, *The Modern Schism: Three Paths to the Secular* (New York: Harper & Row, Publishers, 1969), p. 97.

[25] John Charles Cooper, *Radical Christianity and Its Sources* (Philadelphia: The Westminster Press, 1968), pp. 34-35.

[26] Hans Hoekendijk, "Christ and World in the Modern Age," *The Student World* (Spring, 1961), p. 82.

[27] Williams, *op. cit.*, p. 78.

[28] Hoekendijk, *op. cit.*, p. 75.

[29] Dietrich Bonhoeffer, *Letters and Papers from Prison*, ed. Eberhard Bethge, trans. Reginald H. Fuller (New York: The Macmillan Company, 1962), pp. 162-168.

[30] Cox, *op. cit.*, pp. 4-5.

[31] Daniel Callahan, ed., *The Secular City Debate* (New York: The Macmillan Company, 1966), p. 174.

[32] Martin Marty, *The Search for a Usable Future* (New York: Harper & Row, Publishers, 1969), p. 64.

CHAPTER 4 — THE ECLIPSE OF THE SECULAR

[1] Mircea Eliade, *The Sacred and the Profane: The Nature of Religion*, trans. Willard R. Trask (New York: Harcourt, Brace & World, Inc., 1959), p. 14.

[2] Larry Shiner, "Toward a Theology of Secularization," *The Journal of Religion*, vol. 45 (October, 1965), p. 281.

[3] Paul Tillich, *Systematic Theology*, vol. 1 (Chicago: The University of Chicago Press, 1951), p. 218.

[4] Bernard Meland, *The Secularization of Modern Cultures* (New York: Oxford University Press, 1966), p. 82.

[5] Paul Tillich, *Theology of Culture*, ed. Robert C. Kimball (New York: Oxford University Press, 1959), p. 152.

[6] Shiner, *op. cit.*, p. 282.

[7] *Ibid.*, p. 283, quoting Paul Tillich, *The Protestant Era* (Chicago: Phoenix Books, 1957), p. xi.

[8] Tillich, *Systematic Theology*, vol. 1, p. 84.

[9] *Ibid.*, vol. 3, p. 380.

[10] Meland, *The Secularization of Modern Cultures*, p. 3.

[11] *Ibid.*, p. 33.

[12] Bernard Meland, *The Realities of Faith: The Revolution in Cultural Forms* (New York: Oxford University Press, 1962), p. 64.

[13] *Ibid.*, p. 4.

[14] Eliade, *op. cit.*, p. 203.

[15] *Ibid.*, p. 213.

[16] *Ibid.*, p. 57.

[17] Tillich, *Theology of Culture*, p. 8.

[18] *Ibid.*, p. 9.

[19] *Ibid.*, p. 42.

[20] Meland, *The Secularization of Modern Cultures*, p. 136.

[21] *Ibid.*, p. 20.

[22] Harvey Cox, *The Feast of Fools: A Theological Essay on Festivity and Fantasy* (Cambridge: Harvard University Press, 1969), p. 5.

[23] *Ibid.*, p. viii.

[24] Martin Marty and Dean G. Peerman, eds., *New Theology No. 2* (New York: The Macmillan Company, 1965), p. 27.

CHAPTER 5 — THE DEATH OF THE SACRED

[1] Eric Hoffer, as quoted in Martin Marty, *The Modern*

Schism: Three Paths to the Secular (New York: Harper & Row, Publishers, 1969), p. 9.

² Neitzsche, *Die Frohliche Wissenschaft,* as quoted in Bernard Murchland, ed., *The Meaning of the Death of God: Protestant, Jewish, and Catholic Scholars Explore Atheistic Theology* (New York: Random House, Inc., 1967), p. 81.

³ Langdon Gilkey, *Naming the Whirlwind: The Renewal of God-Language* (Indianapolis: The Bobbs-Merrill Company, 1969), pp. 85-88.

⁴ *Ibid.,* p. 91.

⁵ Gabriel Vahanian, *The Death of God: The Culture of Our Post-Christian Era* (New York: George Braziller, 1957), p. 164.

⁶ Albert Camus, *The Rebel,* trans. Anthony Bower (New York: Alfred A. Knopf, Inc., 1961), p. 21.

⁷ Vahanian, *op. cit.,* p. 13.

⁸ *Ibid.,* p. 187.

⁹ Thomas Altizer and William Hamilton, *Radical Theology and the Death of God* (Indianapolis: The Bobbs-Merrill Company, 1966), pp. 144-153.

¹⁰ Paul Van Buren, *The Secular Meaning of the Gospel: Based on an Analysis of Its Language* (New York: The Macmillan Company, 1963), p. 2.

¹¹ *Ibid.,* p. 81.

¹² T. S. Eliot, "Choruses from 'The Rock' " in *The Complete Poems and Plays* (New York: Harcourt, Brace & World, Inc., 1952), p. 108.

¹³ Martin Buber, *Eclipse of God: Studies in the Relation Between Religion and Philosophy* (New York: Harper & Row, Publishers, 1952), p. 22.

¹⁴ Peter Berger, *A Rumor of Angels: Modern Society and the Rediscovery of the Supernatural* (Garden City, N. Y.: Doubleday & Company, Inc., 1969), p. 1.

¹⁵ Martin Marty, *et al., What Do We Believe?* (Des Moines: Meredith Press, 1968), p. 47.

¹⁶ *Ibid.,* p. 32.

¹⁷ J. V. Langmead Casserley, *The Death of God: A Critique of Christian Atheism* (New York: Morehouse-Barlow Company, 1967), p. 13.

¹⁸ *Ibid.,* p. 20.

¹⁹ *Ibid.*

[20] Altizer and Hamilton, *op. cit.*, p. 28.

[21] J. D. Salinger, *Catcher in the Rye* (New York: Bantam Books, 1964), p. 100.

[22] Gilkey, *op. cit.*, p. 70.

[23] Michael Hamburger, ed., *Holderin* (New York: Pantheon Books, Inc., 1952) as quoted in Harvey Cox, *The Feast of Fools: A Theological Essay on Festivity and Fantasy* (Cambridge: Harvard University Press, 1969), p. 27.

[24] Martin Marty and Dean G. Peerman, eds., *New Theology No. 2* (New York: The Macmillan Company, 1965), p. 47.

[25] *Ibid.*, p. 45.

[26] Vahanian, *op. cit.*, p. 49.

[27] Samuel Beckett, *Waiting for Godot* (New York: Grove Press, 1954), p. 8.

[28] John Charles Cooper, *Radical Christianity and Its Sources* (Philadelphia: The Westminster Press, 1968), p. 29.

CHAPTER 6 — THE SACRED THROUGH THE SECULAR

[1] Langdon Gilkey, *Naming the Whirlwind: The Renewal of God-Language* (Indianapolis: The Bobbs-Merrill Company, 1969), p. 51.

[2] D. L. Munby, *The Idea of a Secular Society: And Its Significance for Christians* (London: Oxford University Press, 1963), p. 25.

[3] C. G. Jung, *Modern Man in Search of a Soul*, trans. W. S. Dell (New York: Harcourt, Brace & World, Inc., 1933), p. 197.

[4] *Ibid.*, pp. 226-227.

[5] Peter Berger, *A Rumor of Angels: Modern Society and the Rediscovery of the Supernatural* (Garden City, N. Y.: Doubleday & Company, Inc., 1969), p. 61.

[6] Gilkey, *op. cit.*, p. 234.

[7] Thomas Luckmann, *The Invisible Religion: The Problem of Religion in Modern Society* (New York: The Macmillan Company, 1967), p. 23.

[8] *Ibid.*, p. 51.

[9] Egbert De Vries, ed., *Man in Community: Christian Concern for the Human in Changing Society* (New York: Association Press, 1966), p. 315.

[10] Martin Marty, *The Modern Schism: Three Paths to the*

Secular (New York: Harper & Row, Publishers, 1969), p. 11.

[11] Luckmann, *op. cit.*, p. 83.

[12] Berger, *op. cit.*, p. 120.

[13] Luckmann, *op. cit.*, p. 54.

[14] Paul Tillich, *Systematic Theology*, vol. 3 (Chicago: The University of Chicago Press, 1951), p. 310.

[15] Johannes B. Metz, *Theology of the World*, trans. William Glen-Doepel (New York: Herder and Herder, 1969), p. 110.

[16] Saul Alinsky, *Reveille for Radicals* (New York: Vintage Books, 1969), p. 18.

[17] Michael Harrington, *Toward a Democratic Left: A Radical Program for a New Majority* (New York: The Macmillan Company, 1968), p. 298.

Bibliography

Alinsky, Saul, *Reveille for Radicals*. New York: Vintage Books, 1969.

Altizer, Thomas, and Hamilton, William, *Radical Theology and the Death of God*. Indianapolis: The Bobbs-Merrill Company, 1966.

Altizer, Thomas, *The Altizer-Montgomery Dialogue*. Chicago: Inter-Varsity Press, 1967.

Aubrey, Edwin, *Secularism a Myth*. New York: Harper & Row, Publishers, 1954.

Banfield, Edward C., and Wilson, James Q., *City Politics*. New York: Vintage Books, 1963.

Beckett, Samuel, *Waiting for Godot*. New York: Grove Press, 1954.

Bennett, John C., ed., *Christian Social Ethics in a Changing World*. New York: Association Press, 1966.

Berger, Peter, *A Rumor of Angels: Modern Society and the Rediscovery of the Supernatural*. Garden City, N. Y.: Doubleday & Company, Inc., 1969.

Blamires, Harry, *The Christian Mind*. New York: The Seabury Press, 1963.

153

Bonhoeffer, Dietrich, *Letters and Papers from Prison*. Edited by Eberhard Bethge. Translated by Reginald H. Fuller. New York: The Macmillan Company, 1962.

Buber, Martin, *Eclipse of God: Studies in the Relation Between Religion and Philosophy*. New York: Harper & Row, Publishers, 1952.

Bultmann, Rudolf, *Jesus Christ and Mythology*. New York: Charles Scribner's Sons, 1958.

—————, *Kerygma and Myth*. Edited by Hans Werner Bartsch. New York: Harper & Row, Publishers, 1961.

Callahan, Daniel, ed., *The Secular City Debate*. New York: The Macmillan Company, 1966.

Camus, Albert, *The Rebel*. Translated by Anthony Bower. New York: Alfred A. Knopf, Inc., 1961.

Casserley, J. V. Langmead, *The Death of God: A Critique of Christian Atheism*. New York: Morehouse-Barlow Company, 1967.

Cherbonnier, E. La B., *Hardness of Heart*. Garden City, N. Y.: Doubleday and Company, Inc., 1955.

Cooper, John Charles, *Radical Christianity and Its Sources*. Philadelphia: The Westminster Press, 1968.

Coser, Lewis A., *The Functions of Social Conflict*. London: Collier-Macmillan, Limited, 1964.

Cox, Harvey, *The Secular City*. New York: The Macmillan Company, 1965.

—————, *The Feast of Fools: A Theological Essay on Festivity and Fantasy*. Cambridge: Harvard University Press, 1969.

Cutler, Donald R., ed., *The Religious Situation: 1968*. Boston: Beacon Press, 1968.

De Vries, Egbert, ed., *Man in Community: Christian Concern for the Human in Changing Society*. New York: Association Press, 1966.

Dewart, Leslie, *The Future of Belief*. New York: Herder and Herder, 1966.

Eliade, Mircea, *The Sacred and the Profane: The Nature of Religion*. Translated by Willard R. Trask. New York: Harcourt, Brace & World, Inc., 1959.

Eliot, T. S., *The Idea of a Christian Society*. New York: Harcourt, Brace & World, Inc., 1940.

Ellul, Jacques, *The Technological Society*. Translated by John Wilkinson. New York: Alfred A. Knopf, Inc., 1964.

—————, *The Presence of the Kingdom*. London: SCM Press, 1951.

Gilkey, Langdon, *Naming the Whirlwind: The Renewal of God-Language*. Indianapolis: The Bobbs-Merrill Company, 1969.

Hamilton, Kenneth, *God Is Dead: The Anatomy of a Slogan*. Grand Rapids: William B. Eerdmans Publishing Company, 1966.

Harrington, Michael, *Toward a Democratic Left: A Radical Program for a New Majority*. New York: The Macmillan Company, 1968.

Jarrett-Kerr, Martin, *The Secular Promise*. Philadelphia: Fortress Press, 1964.

Jung, C. G., *Modern Man in Search of a Soul*. Translated by W. S. Dell and Cary F. Baynes. New York: Harcourt, Brace & World, Inc., 1939.

Kallen, Horace M., *Secularism Is the Will of God*. New York: Twayne Publishers, 1954.

Kierkegaard, Soren, *Kierkegaard's Attack upon "Christendom."* Translated by Walter Lowrie. Boston: Beacon Press, 1944.

Lenski, Gerhard, *The Religious Factor*. Garden City, N. Y.: Doubleday and Company, Inc., 1963.

Lipset, Seymour Martin, *Political Man*. Garden City, N. Y.: Doubleday and Company, Inc., 1963.

Luckmann, Thomas, *The Invisible Religion: The Problem of Religion in Modern Society*. New York: The Macmillan Company, 1967.

Marty, Martin, ed., *New Theology No. 1*. New York: The Macmillan Company, 1964.

—————, *New Theology No. 2*. New York: The Macmillan Company, 1965.

—————, *New Theology No. 3*. New York: The Macmillan Company, 1966.

—————, *New Theology No. 4*. New York: The Macmillan Company, 1967.

—————, *New Theology No. 5*. New York: The Macmillan Company, 1968.

————————, *New Theology No. 6*. New York: The Macmillan Company, 1969.

————————, *The Place of Bonhoeffer*. New York: Association Press, 1962.

————————, *The Modern Schism: Three Paths to the Secular*. New York: Harper & Row, Publishers, 1969.

————————, *The Search for a Usable Future*. New York: Harper & Row, Publishers, 1969.

Marty, Martin, *et al.*, *What Do We Believe?* Des Moines: Meredith Press, 1968.

May, Herbert G., ed., *The Holy Bible*. New York: Oxford University Press, 1962.

Meland, Bernard, *The Realities of Faith: The Revolution of Cultural Forms*. New York: Oxford University Press, 1962.

————————, *The Secularization of Modern Cultures*. New York: Oxford University Press, 1966.

Metz, Johannes B., *Theology of the World*. Translated by William Glen-Doepel. New York: Herder and Herder, 1969.

Micklem, Philip Arthur, *The Secular and the Sacred*. London: Hodder and Stoughton, Limited, 1948.

Munby, D. L., ed., *Economic Growth in World Perspective*. New York: Association Press, 1966.

————————, *The Idea of a Secular Society: And Its Significance for Christians*. London: Oxford University Press, 1963.

Murchland, Bernard, ed., *The Meaning of the Death of God*. New York: Vintage Books, 1967.

Newbigin, Lesslie, *Honest Religion for Secular Man*. Philadelphia: The Westminster Press, 1966.

Niebuhr, Richard H., *Christ and Culture*. New York: Harper & Row, Publishers, 1951.

Peck, William George, *Christianity and the Modern Chaos*. New York: Morehouse-Barlow Co., Inc., 1934.

Shiner, Larry, *The Secularization of History: An Introduction to the Theology of Friedrich Gogarten*. Nashville: Abingdon Press, 1966.

Smith, Ronald G., *Secular Christianity*. London: Collins, 1966.

Tillich, Paul, *Biblical Religion and the Search for Ultimate Reality*. Chicago: The University of Chicago Press, 1964.

————————, *Systematic Theology*. 3 vols. Chicago: The University of Chicago Press, 1951-1963.

_____, *Theology of Culture*. New York: Oxford University Press, 1964.

Todrank, Gustave H., *The Secular Search for a New Christ*. Philadelphia: The Westminster Press, 1969.

Vahanian, Gabriel, *The Death of God: The Culture of Our Post-Christian Era*. New York: George Braziller, Inc., 1957.

Van Buren, Paul, *The Secular Meaning of the Gospel: Based on an Analysis of Its Language*. New York: The Macmillan Company, 1963.

Van Leeuwen, Arend Th., *Christianity in World History: The Meeting of the Faiths of East and West*. Translated by H. H. Hoskins. London: Edinburgh House Press, 1964.

Von Weizsäcker, C. F., *The Relevance of Science: Creation and Cosmogony*. London: Collins, 1964.

Washington, Joseph R., *The Politics of God*. Boston: Beacon Press, 1967.

Weber, Max, *Politics as a Vocation*. Translated by H. H. Gerth and C. Wright Mills. Philadelphia: Fortress Press, 1965.

White, Winston, *Beyond Conformity*. New York: The Free Press of Glencoe, Inc., 1961.

Williams, Colin, *Faith in a Secular Age*. New York: Harper & Row, Publishers, 1966.

Winter, Gibson, *The New Creation as Metropolis*. New York: The Macmillan Company, 1963.

_____, *The Suburban Captivity of the Churches*. New York: The Macmillan Company, 1962.

PERIODICALS

Adams, James L., "The Law of Nature in Greco-Roman Thought," *The Journal of Religion*, vol. 25 (April, 1945), pp. 97-118.

Deschner, J., "Christian Students and the Challenge of Our Times," *The Student World*, vol. 54 (Spring, 1961), pp. 83-95.

"Evangelical Springtime," *The Christian Century* (1967), p. 575, as quoted from the University of Minnesota's *Minnesota Daily* (February 14, 1967).

Hoekendijk, Hans, "Christ and the World in the Modern Age," *The Student World*, vol. 54 (Spring, 1961), pp. 75-82.

Jarrett-Kerr, Martin, "The Secular: Substitute, Challenge, or

Heir-Apparent?" *Religion in Life,* vol. 35 (Winter, 1965-1966), pp. 20-30.

Mackie, S., "European Christians and the Secular Debate," *The Student World,* vol. 56 (Spring, 1963), pp. 4-12.

Meland, Bernard, "Alternatives to Absolutes," *Religion in Life,* vol. 34 (Summer, 1965), pp. 343-352.

Niebuhr, Rheinhold, "The King's Chapel and the King's Court," *Christianity and Crisis* (August 4, 1969), p. 212.

Schroeder, W. W., "The Secular City: A Critique," *Religion in Life,* vol. 35 (Autumn, 1966), pp. 504-512.

Shiner, Larry, "Toward a Theology of Secularization," *The Journal of Religion,* vol. 45 (October, 1965), pp. 279-295.

Van Buren, Paul, "The Dissolution of the Absolute," *Religion in Life,* vol. 34 (Summer, 1965), pp. 334-343.

Van Peursen, Cornelius A., "Man and Reality — The History of Human Thought," *The Student World* (Spring, 1963), pp. 13-29.

West, Charles C., "Theological Table-Talk," *Theology Today,* vol. 23 (October, 1966), pp. 417-427.

Index

261
S+9